Hermeneutics as a General Methodology of the Sciences of the Spirit

With a Foreword by Lars Vinx, this book is the first complete English translation of the Italian jurist, Emilio Betti's classic work *Die Hermeneutik als allgemeine Methodik der Geisteswissenschaften*, originally published in 1962.

Betti's hermeneutical theory is presented here as a 'general methodology of the sciences of the spirit', such as to allow the achievement of objectivity, however relative it might be. Its central focus is the tension between an object, to be considered in its autonomy, and the subjectivity of the interpreter, who can understand the object only by means of his or her own categories, historical-cultural conditions, and interests. Set against the work of Bultmann and Gadamer, Betti is concerned to limit the arbitrariness of subjectivity without diminishing the place of interpretation. Detailing the principles that govern, and therefore, guide any interpretation, Betti traces how interpretation in art and in literature, as well as in the fields of science, jurisprudence, sociology, and economy, can be said to be objective, albeit only ever in a relative sense.

This summa of Betti's key contribution to hermeneutic theory will be of interest across a range of disciplines, including legal and literary theory, philosophy, as well as the history and sociology of law.

Emilio Betti (1890–1968) was an Italian jurist, Roman Law scholar and philosopher.

Part of the
LAW AND POLITICS: CONTINENTAL PERSPECTIVES
series

series editors
Mariano Croce, *Sapienza University of Rome, Italy*
Marco Goldoni, *University of Glasgow, UK*

for information about the series and details of previousand forthcoming titles, see
https://www.routledge.com/law/series/LPCP

A GlassHouse book

Hermeneutics as a General Methodology of the Sciences of the Spirit

Emilio Betti

a GlassHouse Book

First published 2021
by Routledge
2 Park Square, Milton Park, Abingdon, Oxon OX14 4RN

and by Routledge
52 Vanderbilt Avenue, New York, NY 10017

a GlassHouse book

Routledge is an imprint of the Taylor & Francis Group, an informa business

© 2021 Emilio Betti

The right of Emilio Betti to be identified as author of this work has been asserted by him in accordance with sections 77 and 78 of the Copyright, Designs and Patents Act 1988.

All rights reserved. No part of this book may be reprinted or reproduced or utilised in any form or by any electronic, mechanical, or other means, now known or hereafter invented, including photocopying and recording, or in any information storage or retrieval system, without permission in writing from the publishers.

Trademark notice: Product or corporate names may be trademarks or registered trademarks, and are used only for identification and explanation without intent to infringe.

Published in German by J.C.B. Mohr, 1962

British Library Cataloguing-in-Publication Data
A catalogue record for this book is available from the British Library

Library of Congress Cataloging-in-Publication Data
A catalog record has been requested for this book

ISBN: 978-0-367-48136-0 (hbk)
ISBN: 978-0-367-74334-5 (pbk)
ISBN: 978-1-003-15723-6 (ebk)

Typeset in Bembo
by Spi Global, India

As the president of the Emilio Betti Institute, I am naturally very happy with this English translation of the book that Betti wrote in German in 1962 (while the one translated here is the 1972 second edition). I would like to thank Mariano Croce and Marco Goldoni, the series editors of Law & Politics: Continental Perspectives. They first had the idea of making this key work of Betti's available to an Anglophone audience and turned to the Institute for making it happen. A heartfelt thanks also goes to Giorgio A. Pinton, who accepted the difficult task of translating the book, and to Luca Vargiu, who at any moment was ready to lend his learned help. To Pinton and Vargiu, to all members of the Institute and to me, it is particularly welcome to dedicate this publication to the memory of Giuliano Crifò.

Rome, 18 July 2020
Luca Loschiavo
President of the Istituto Emilio Betti
di Scienza e Teoria del Diritto nella storia e
nella società

Contents

Emilio Betti: A Short Biography		ix
Some Untidy Reflections on the Betti–Gadamer Debate		xi
LARS VINX		
Editorial Preface		xxvi
GIORGIO A. PINTON		

1. Hermeneutical problematics in contemporary consciousness ... 1
2. Objectivations of the spirit ... 4
3. Representative forms ... 5
4. Representative function & expressive value ... 7
5. To Interpret and to understand ... 9
6. The act of interpretation as a triadic process ... 10
7. Inversion of the creative process and transposition into one another subjectivity ... 12
8. The directives of interpretation: The canon of the hermeneutical autonomy of the object ... 14
9. The canon of the coherence of meanings (The Principle of Totality) ... 16

10	Analogy and integrative development	19
11	Canon of the actuality of understanding	21
12	Vital Rapport with the subject-matter & the direction of the inquiry	22
13	Is it possible to achieve the objectivity of the historical phenomena?	25
14	Function of the sensibility for the values proper of the historian: The value-relating interpretation	27
15	The answer to the proposed historical question	30
16	Meaning of a historical phenomenon and its significance in the present	32
17	Dialog and monolog	34
18	Historical interpretation and attribution of an eschatological meaning	36
19	The threat of denying the objectivity	40
20	Theological hermeneutic and demythologizing of the Kerygma	42
21	Recent turn toward the historicity of understanding	45
22	The prejudices as the conditions of the understanding	47
23	Existential foundation of the hermeneutic circle	49
24	The problem of the correctness of the understanding	51
25	Historical understanding as mediation of past and present	55

26 Claim of a practical application of interpretation 57

27 The mentioned claim is justified only if the interpretation is normatively oriented 58

28 Canon of the hermeneutical correspondence of meaning (Adequation of meaning in understanding) 62

29 The character as a work of historical forms of life: Proposes a problematics of the higher grade 64

30 The technical morphologic interpretation in rapport to the prospected problems of formation 66

31 Context of meanings and styles as products of the autonomy of the spiritual human faculties 69

Index 73

Emilio Betti: A Short Biography

Born in Camerino (central Italy) in 1890 and dying in Camorciano (near Camerino) in 1968, Emilio Betti was one of the greatest Italian jurists of the 20th century. His family was the typical of the small landowners in central Italy. His father was a doctor, and his brother, Ugo (1892–1953), became a quite famous poet and playwright.

Although much drawn to history and philosophy (as a young student he would read Vico, Croce, Gentile and – directly in German – Kant, Hegel, Schelling, Fichte, Dilthey and the much-appreciated Nietzsche), he graduated in law in 1912 with a dissertation on obligations in Roman law (1912 he also graduated in History).

Attracted by the academic career (and after two burning disappointments in 1914 and 1915: in both circumstances the commissioners judged his works 'too historical' and 'not quite dogmatic'), Betti obtained the chair of Roman law in the Law Faculty of Macerata in 1917. He then taught in Messina (1924–1925), Florence (1926, where he gave his famous paper on 'The creation of law in the *jurisdictio* of the roman *praetor*') and Milan (from 1927). In those years he expanded his interest, especially in procedure (both Roman and contemporary) and international-comparative law. During this time he published a series of important works, the most famous of which is his *Teoria generale del negozio giuridico*, in which he condemns the *Willensdogma* ('dogma of the will') at that time generally accepted by the continental jurists, in favour of a greater evaluation of the 'cause' and 'function' of the transaction: in other words, Betti affirms the superior importance of the (national) community over private individual interests.

At a relatively early stage, Betti accepted the ideas of fascism; however, he only enrolled in the PNF (National Fascist Party) in 1932 (later he would also join the Republic of Salò). Arrested in 1944, and excluded from teaching in 1945, he was acquitted of all charges in 1946. Despite the strong opposition of some colleagues, in November of that year he was offered the chair of Civil Law at the Law Faculty of the Sapienza University of Rome, where he remained until his retirement in 1960, becoming a point of reference for many future jurists of the Republican Italy.

His years teaching in Rome were very intense and productive ones. In addition to teaching civil law and then Roman law, Betti began to devote himself intensely to the study and teaching of hermeneutics. In 1955 he published his perhaps most successful volume, *The General Theory of Interpretation*, and also founded the Institute of Theory of Interpretation in Rome, and his teaching was included in the order of studies within the Faculty of Law. A very important dialectical confrontation with the German philosopher Hans-Georg Gadamer then began; and Betti and Gadamer still represent the two cornerstones of modern hermeneutic philosophy.

Some Untidy Reflections on the Betti–Gadamer Debate

Lars Vinx

The debate between Emilio Betti and Hans-Georg Gadamer[1] – a debate that began with Betti's attack on Gadamer's hermeneutics in the text presented in English translation in this volume – is characterized by a surprising reversal of role. Betti, the jurist, defended a conception of hermeneutics as a general method of the human sciences, one that takes inspiration from the hermeneutical strategies of what Germans call *Geschichtswissenschaft*, the science of history, and which treats juristic hermeneutics as a mere special case. The philosopher Gadamer, on the other hand, argued that the structure of all hermeneutics, properly understood, is juristic. Juristic hermeneutics interprets norms that purport to set down how we, as subjects of the law, are to behave. If we assume that the law has authority over us, the results of juristic hermeneutics will tell us what it is that we have an obligation to do. Historical hermeneutics, as Betti portrays it, taking his cues from Schleiermacher and Dilthey, has altogether different aims. Its interest is ultimately theoretical, not practical. It aims to achieve a correct understanding of the meaning of acts of expression produced by historical actors, whether these be verbal, written, or consist in mere behaviour, so as to arrive at a descriptively accurate account of the past. It aims to find out, in Ranke's famous words, 'how things actually were'.[2]

---

1 See Emilio Betti, *Hermeneutik als allgemeine Methodik der Geisteswissenschaften* (Tübingen: Mohr Siebeck, 1962), pp. 38–52 [pp. 45–61 in this volume] as well as the response in: Hans-Georg Gadamer, 'Hermeneutik und Historismus', in Hans-Georg Gadamer, *Wahrheit und Methode*, vol. 2: *Ergänzungen* (Tübingen: Mohr Siebeck, 1993), pp. 387–424, at pp. 392–395.
2 Leopold von Ranke, *Geschichten der romanischen und germanischen Völker von 1494-1535*, vol. I (Leipzig and Berlin: G. Reimer, 1824), pp. ix–x [my translation]: 'Some have endowed history with the task to pass judgment on the past, and to educate the world for the benefit of years to come. The present essay does not lay claim to an office as high as this: it only wants to say how things actually were.'

What is at stake in the debate between Betti and Gadamer, in the first instance, or so the jurist argues, is the very possibility of a science of history and of human sciences in general. Betti, like the key proponents of the German romantic hermeneutical tradition he champions, is of course well aware that history, if it is to be a science, must be a science unlike the natural sciences. It does not discover natural laws that would allow us to predict future events, given certain initial conditions, or to explain past events by subsuming them under exceptionless causal regularities. It recognizes that much of the material it investigates, unlike natural objects and events, is meaningful, as it is the product of intentional human action and, in many cases, of explicit communicative behaviour. The method of the science of history must therefore be hermeneutic as opposed to causal-explanatory. Its claim to the status of a science hinges on its ability to nevertheless attain knowledge of the past that is objective, in the sense that Ranke alludes to. If history is to be a science it must be able to tell us 'how things actually were', and not merely how we would have liked them to be, or how we assume they must have been, given the interests we have and the convictions we hold.

If history is to be scientific, Betti believes, it will need to employ a hermeneutical method that leads to accurate understanding of the meaning of the perceivable representative forms which the historian encounters in the course of their research, an understanding that is untainted by prejudices, biases, and practical interests which the interpreter himself might be tempted to read into the historical source.[3] The historian's goal must be to reconstruct as exactly as possible, in his own mind, the semantic content that the historical agent in question intended to express. Objectively correct understanding is achieved, Betti claims, in case the mental process of understanding an utterance, a meaningful gesture, or a written statement, in the mind of the interpreter, constitutes an exact reversal of the productive process in the mind of the speaker, writer, or agent whose meaningful acts are to be understood.[4]

According to Betti, representative forms have meaning because they express thoughts in the mind of their producer. What meaning they have, Betti suggests, is in all cases an objective matter of fact, since it is a matter of objective fact what ideational content the producer of a representative form intended to convey with it. It follows that there is always a fact of the matter for an interpretation to be right or wrong about. An interpretation either manages to accurately capture, to reproduce in the mind of the interpreter,

---

[3] See the discussion of Bultmann's hermeneutics in Betti, *Hermeneutik als allgemeine Methode* (n. 1), pp. 22–35 [pp. 25–41].
[4] See ibid., pp. 7–13 [pp. 11–22].

the intended sense of an expression or it does not. Ranke's idea of the objectivity of the science of history, in this view, translates straightforwardly to hermeneutics. An interpreter's goal is to not to judge or to learn from the thoughts of those whose expressions he seeks to understand, but to find out what they actually thought.

As should be evident, it will often be difficult for the historian to accomplish this task of understanding; s/he may be confronted with very fragmentary remains, produced by human beings who lived in a very different world and held beliefs and convictions very different from her own. Betti's general hermeneutics responds to this difficulty with the promise that there is a method or technique of interpretation which, though it cannot guarantee accurate reproductive understanding, will nevertheless facilitate the achievement of such understanding. In the text presented here, Betti summarizes that method, by laying out four fundamental canons of hermeneutics.

The first of these is the canon of the hermeneutical *autonomy* of the object of interpretation.[5] The objects of interpretation are to be understood according to the law of their own formation, that is, in the context in which they were produced, and in accordance with the intentions and purposes of the producer, whom Betti refers to as a 'demiurge', and not in light of an extrinsic purpose that might suggest itself to the interpreter.[6] The canon of autonomy, as should be clear, flows from a demand for objectivity of understanding. Meaning is not to be imposed on the object by the interpreter. Rather, the interpreter is to find the meaning the producer of the object intended to express.

Betti's second canon of interpretation, the canon of *totality*, addresses the circular structure of interpretation.[7] It demands that the meaning of any particular object of interpretation be elucidated in its proper context. A particular spoken phrase, a written sentence or sentence-fragment, a particular gesture form part of a wider discourse, of a larger text, or a more extended performance. Though the meaning to be attributed to the discourse, the text, or the performance as a whole depends on the meaning of its constituent parts, the meaning of the constituent parts, in turn, can only be determined in light of the meaning of the whole. Our assumptions about the meaning of the whole and the parts must inform each other, they must, at the end of the process of interpretation, to borrow a Rawlsian phrase, stand in reflective equilibrium. Any application of the canon of totality in the process of interpretation, needless to say, will have to

---

5 See ibid., pp. 14–15 [pp. 25–26].
6 See ibid.
7 See ibid., pp. 15–19 [pp. 27–33].

determine which context, precisely, is relevant for achieving the best possible understanding of a particular representative form. In line with the romantic tradition from which he takes inspiration, Betti argues that the ultimate context within which any particular representative form is to be interpreted is the totality of the life of the mind of the person who produced it. It is this biographical context that must be privileged if we assume that the task of interpretation is to reproduce the content of the expressive intention of the producer of a representative form in the mind of the interpreter.

The third canon is that of the *actuality* of understanding.[8] It acknowledges that interpretation cannot be purely passive. Successful reconstruction of the meaning expressed in a historical source requires that the interpreter be able to relate the content of that source to his or her own experiential background. She is called upon to translate it into the actuality of her own life through an effort of sympathetic understanding. The canon of actuality contains a concession that understanding cannot be presuppositionless. To understand, say, a philosophical or legal text, we must be able to reason with the ideas expressed in it, to see how they might be applied to cases, scenarios, or instances not explicitly discussed in the text itself. To understand meaningful behaviour, we must be able to understand what purposes or ends it might have been intended to serve, which requires that we be able to attribute purposes and ends to the general pattern of observed behaviour that we are to interpret. This task of sympathetic identification will hardly be possible unless the interpreter can recognize the object to be interpreted as the product of the activity of an agent whose beliefs, concerns, and goals are intelligible to the interpreter.

The fourth and last of Betti's hermeneutic canons, that of *adequacy* of meaning,[9] builds on the insight that an interpreter must be able to put himself into the shoes of the person whose speech, writings, or behaviour are to be understood. Betti's description of this canon has clear moral undertones. What is required for successful interpretation, he argues, is not merely that the interpreter have a desire to understand. It is necessary, in addition, that the interpreter exhibit 'a spiritual open-mindedness' as well as 'unselfishness and humble self-effacement, as they are manifested in the sincere and decisive overcoming of personal prejudices'.[10] In effect, the canon of adequacy is the subjective equivalent, on the interpreter's side, of the first canon of the hermeneutical autonomy of the object of interpretation. It demands a frame

---

8 See ibid., p. 19–20 [p. 21].
9 See ibid., pp. 53–54 [pp. 62–63].
10 Ibid., p. 53 [p. 62].

of mind that enables the interpreter to respect the autonomy of the object, to listen to what the source has to say.

Betti's four canons of interpretation, obviously, are not free of internal tension. The third canon, that of the actuality of understanding, in particular, puts pressure on the demand to respect the hermeneutical autonomy of the object of interpretation (as well as its subjective counterpart, the demand for adequacy of understanding), and thus on the ideal of objectivity that Betti's hermeneutics is intended to safeguard. This tension comes to the fore most visibly in juristic hermeneutics. At first glance, this claim might be surprising. Juristic hermeneutics, after all, is concerned, paradigmatically, with the interpretation of laws, with statutory commands, enacted by a sovereign lawgiver who is assumed to have the authority to enact rules subjects are bound to obey. What could be more important, in this context, than to make sure that the meaning of the objects of interpretation is understood in precisely the way the producer intended them to be understood?

The problem, of course, is that laws are general commands that require application, to cases not foreseen by the legislator or not explicitly regulated in the statutory command. Even Hobbes, when addressing the problem of legal interpretation, was forced to admit that juristic hermeneutics must rely on an idealizing method that does not aim to track the actual psychological intentions of the lawgiver, but rather to ensure that the application of laws to particular cases leads to reasonable outcomes: 'The Intention of the Legislator is always supposed to be equity: For it were a great contumely for a Judge to think otherwise of the Soveraigne.'[11] What is required of the interpreting judge, in this view, is much more than a sympathetic but respectful engagement with the actual intention of the legislator. Since it is the legislator's task to implement basic practical principles that Hobbes calls the 'laws of nature', a judge must interpret laws as though they were made with that intention, and then apply them in light of his best understanding of what the laws of nature do, in fact, require. To do otherwise would be disrespectful to the sovereign, as it would suggest that the sovereign's actual intention differs from the intention that flows from a proper understanding of sovereign role. It should be clear that Hobbes's view of juristic interpretation violates the canon of the hermeneutical autonomy of the object that is to be interpreted, and this violation is only more pronounced in some influential modern accounts of juristic interpretation. Dworkin's interpretivism explicitly claims that juristic interpretation must attribute to some legal practice that point or purpose which is best suited to morally justify

---

11 Thomas Hobbes, *Leviathan*, ed. Richard Tuck (Cambridge: Cambridge University Press, 1991), p. 194.

the coercion-backed decisions produced by legal institutions, irrespective of what the actual intention of the legislator might have been.[12] Juristic hermeneutics, so understood, clearly cannot be objective in anything like the Rankean sense.

A defender of a scientific hermeneutics will respond by pointing out that juristic hermeneutics is a special case, for the reason that the demand for actuality of understanding takes a peculiar form in the juristic context.[13] We apply legal rules not merely to satisfy our theoretical interest in understanding what they mean or what their producer intended. We do so to determine what it is that we are legally obligated to do. The law makes a claim, according to both Hobbes and Dworkin, to be morally justified in imposing its demands on us. The legal interpreter assumes, that is, that the fact that the law demands of its subjects that they act in a certain way suffices to put those subjects under an obligation so to act, even before threats of punishment come into consideration. To interpret the law from an idealizing perspective that engages the interpreter's own convictions as to what purposes it would be reasonable for law to pursue is necessary to sustain the law's normative claims. But this pull towards a practical perspective does not hold, it might be argued, if the interpreter's aim is merely to understand, as accurately as possible, the meaning the producer of a representative form intended to express. In historical research, we simply want to find out 'how things actually were', and we do not attribute any practical (or, for that matter, theoretical) authority to the sources that we aim to understand in order to give ourselves an objective picture of the past.

It is at this point, as I pointed out at the beginning, that Gadamer and Betti clash head-on. Gadamer thinks that juristic hermeneutics provides a general model of interpretation, though his understanding of juristic interpretation differs in some important respects, as we shall see, from Hobbes's or Dworkin's. What makes juristic hermeneutics a general model, Gadamer argues, is precisely that it explicitly recognizes that understanding involves application.[14] Gadamer argues that to understand an object of interpretation aright always requires a critical engagement on the part of the interpreter, an engagement in which the interpreter will have to evaluate (and perhaps to re-evaluate) both his or her own convictions and those expressed in the source.

The gist of Gadamer's position, which cannot be discussed here in all its details, can be brought out by focusing on a claim to which Betti takes

---

12 See Ronald Dworkin, *Law's Empire* (London: Fontana Press, 1986).
13 See Betti, *Hermeneutik als allgemeine Methode* (n. 1), pp. 48–52 [pp. 57–61].
14 See Hans-Georg Gadamer, *Truth and Method*, transl. by Joel Weinsheimer and Donald G. Marshall (London and New York: Continuum Press, 2004), pp. 320–355.

particularly strong exception. In presenting his understanding of the problem of the hermeneutic circle, Gadamer argues that any interpretive endeavour must be guided by what he calls a '*Vorgriff der Vollkommenheit*' or anticipation of perfection.[15] Gadamer's hermeneutic circle is not to be understood, as in Betti's canon of totality, as a relationship between the parts and the whole of the discourse, text, or life that is to be interpreted. It involves the interpreter's beliefs and convictions. To understand the object of interpretation, we must assume that it is understandable to us, that is, that it has been created and been endowed with meaning by an agent whose beliefs, convictions and intentions are intelligible to us. The interpreter and the agent whose expressions are to be understood must therefore belong to a common horizon, to a historical continuum or tradition that is characterized by the fact that both the interpreter and the agent share a fair number of beliefs and convictions about the world and about what is valuable and interesting. It is only on the basis of the assumption that there are such shared beliefs that it is possible for the interpreter to anticipate the meaning of the discourse or text that they are to understand, and without such anticipations the process of interpretation cannot get going. Gadamer concludes that 'the prejudice of completeness, then, implies not only [...] that a text should completely express its meaning – but also that what it says should be the complete truth'.[16] This anticipation of truth can only ever be partially disappointed, Gadamer claims, if understanding is to be possible at all. To disagree with a source or to question the truth of one of her claims is possible only against a background of far-reaching implicit agreement.

Instances in which the anticipation of perfection is partially disappointed are nevertheless of pivotal importance for Gadamer. They are opportunities, he thinks, to test our own convictions and beliefs by way of confrontation with the tradition's claims. We may find, in some cases, that the claims made by the source are, from our point of view, misguided or irrelevant, to be explained away historically, by the use of the techniques of textual critique or of historical psychology or sociology. But Gadamer argues that some claims that are implicit in the tradition and that stick in our craw will turn out to be justified and to survive our critical questioning. We must therefore be ready to learn from and to defer to the authority of tradition, to abandon some of our own beliefs and convictions in an encounter with the object of interpretation. The encounter with the tradition, then, affords us with the opportunity to test and to slowly transform our own prejudices. But this

---

15 Ibid., p. 294. The English version of *Wahrheit und Methode* translates 'Vorgriff der Vollkommenheit' as 'fore-conception of completeness'.
16 Ibid.

process must be piecemeal if it is not to foreclose the very possibility of understanding.[17]

We can now see in what sense Gadamer can be said to generalize the model of juristic hermeneutics to all interpretation. For us to be able to understand the object of interpretation, Gadamer thinks, we must attribute epistemic and, in case the source makes practical claims, practical authority to the tradition. As has already been pointed out, Gadamer does not argue that the claims of tradition are beyond criticism. Any criticism of the claims of tradition, however, will have to be interstitial. That we acknowledge that the claims of tradition are by and large true is a condition of the very possibility of adequate understanding. Just as the juristic interpreter must presume that the claims of the law are reasonable, so the historical interpreter must presume that the claims of tradition are accurate. The anticipation of perfection thus corresponds to the juristic assumption that the laws enacted by a sovereign conform to the law of nature or, to put it in Dworkinian terms, that the decisions that flow from a legal practice can be given an interpretation under which the public violence these decisions license turns out to be morally justified.

It should be noted, however, that Gadamer's adaptation puts a particular twist on the juristic model. To bring out that twist, let us consider again Hobbes's claim that an interpreter must assume that the legislator intends to enact legal rules which are equitable. Hobbes is decidedly not of the opinion that the question whether some rule enacted by the sovereign can, indeed, be regarded as equitable is to be regarded as settled by the fact that the rule in question has been enacted by the sovereign or been laid down in precedent.[18] Though a judicial interpreter of the positive law would, of course, have to defer to the sovereign's authority should the latter, in his capacity as supreme judge, decide a doubtful case himself, for the reason that deference to direct instructions issued by the sovereign is a condition of the preservation of the state and the avoidance of civil war, sovereign authority – or, for that matter, the authority of precedent – can never, in Hobbes's view, make a substantively inequitable decision equitable. Interpreters are to use what wiggle room they have to make sure that, going forward, legal practice comes to approximate true equity, as determined by practice-independent standards of natural law, ever more closely. The interpreter's understanding of these standards is not to be defined by tradition, by past judicial and legislative decisions. Deference to positive law, whether it be statutory or take the form of precedent, is to be demanded only on pragmatic grounds. Positive law exercises a settlement-function that is

---

17 See ibid., pp. 278–285.
18 See Hobbes, *Leviathan* (n. 11), pp. 192–195.

conducive to social peace. But the interpreter is not to assume, as Gadamer would have it, that the value judgments expressed in past decisions are to be presumed to be true for the reason that they have become embedded in a historically extended legal practice or tradition. Gadamer denies, while Hobbes affirms, that there are practice independent standards of moral judgment, standards that are not themselves presupposed by and interstitially tested and refined in the hermeneutical process. As we have seen, Gadamer is careful not to advocate for a runic traditionalism, but his view is much closer to the ideology of the common law that Hobbes was concerned to attack than to the model of juristic hermeneutics one finds in Hobbes, or, for that matter, in Dworkin.

We will have to return to this difference in conceptions of juristic hermeneutics at a later point. For now, we need to note that Gadamer's understanding of juristic hermeneutics is as inimical to Betti's general hermeneutics as Hobbes's or Dworkin's more radically constructive approach. Both require the juristic interpreter to violate the canon of the hermeneutic autonomy of the object and to enter into a critical and evaluative interrogation of the object of interpretation, so as to ensure that the outcomes of the process of application have contemporary relevance and are defensible as true. If Gadamer is right to argue that all interpretation, and not merely the interpretation of legal materials for purposes of application, must follow this scheme, then there can be no objective, detached understanding of the sort of advocated by Betti's general hermeneutics. In trying to understand, we can never merely try to find out what it is that the producer of a signifier wanted to express. We can never answer that latter question without entering into a dialogue that raises the question of the truth of both our own claims and of the claims of the historical source that is to be understood.

In the work presented here, Betti aims to defend general hermeneutics, as a method of the human sciences, against precisely this challenge, in a lengthy excursus on Gadamer's argument in *Truth and Method*.[19] It cannot be said, however, that the considerations that Betti puts forward to address Gadamer's critique of general hermeneutics are altogether compelling.

The main reply Betti makes to Gadamer is to argue, in effect, that if an interpreter does not follow the four canons, they will not be able to attain objective understanding, of the sort that could sustain a claim that the humanities are sciences. In Betti's analysis, Gadamer's hermeneutics, and in particular the anticipation of perfection, carries the danger of eliding the difference between finding and imposing meaning and is thus likely to encourage violations of the canons of hermeneutic autonomy as well as (on

---

19 See Betti, *Hermeneutik als allgemeine Methode* (n. 1), pp. 38–52 [pp. 45–61].

the side of the interpreter) of hermeneutic adequacy. Gadamer's hermeneutics, Betti suggests, will simply have the interpreter read his or her own values or beliefs into the object that is to be interpreted. As a result, its outcomes must fail to understand the source in its own terms, in terms that accurately reconstruct the intentions of the producer. Betti makes it clear, in a discussion of Bultmann's existentialist theological hermeneutics, that he is not so naïve as to fail to recognize that the hermeneutical process inevitably engages the interpreter's practical interests. Appealing to the authority of Max Weber, Betti concedes that the interpreter's interests usually guide the choice for and the delimitation of a particular subject of hermeneutical inquiry, but he argues, like Weber, that such judgments of relevance need not undermine the hermeneutical distance between interpreter and object of interpretation that is demanded by the four canons.[20]

These responses to Gadamer are problematic for at least two reasons. The charge that Gadamer undermines the distinction between finding and imposing meaning, and thus undercuts the possibility of suitably detached and objective understanding, would appear to beg the question against Gadamer. Gadamer argues, to recall, that understanding, the attribution of meaning, is possible only on the basis of far-reaching agreement in belief between the interpreter and the source. If the anticipation of perfection was to run into systematic disappointment in the attempt to understand, the interpreter would simply be unable to attribute meaning to the source. Shared prejudices are a condition of the possibility of successful communication. If that claim is true, it follows, apparently, that the distinction between finding and imposing meaning is unsustainable, at least if it is meant to be understood in a suitably radical way that suggests that full understanding is possible under conditions of complete detachment from the truth-claims made in a source. To argue against Gadamer, one would have to show that the latter's portrayal of the conditions of the possibility of understanding is mistaken, and Betti does not offer any critique along those lines. The appeal to Weber flounders for the same reason. Weber may well have been right to argue that the fact that practical interests determine what questions a social scientist will ask does not entail that the answers to those questions must themselves vary with the interpreter's values. But that insight falls short of a response to Gadamer's argument, as the latter is concerned, ultimately, with the conditions of the very possibility of linguistic understanding.

---

20 See ibid., pp. 24–27 [pp. 27–29]. Betti's reference is to Max Weber, 'Roscher und Knies und die logischen Probleme der historischen Nationalökonomie', in Max Weber, *Gesammelte Aufsätze zur Wissenschaftslehre*, ed. by Johannes Winckelmann (Tübingen: Mohr Siebeck, 1951), pp. 1–145, at pp. 119–122.

Betti's charge that Gadamer's hermeneutics will lead the interpreter to impose meaning on the source, though it is ostensibly driven by a concern for objectivity of understanding, has certain moral undertones that echo the romantic dissatisfaction with the historiography of the enlightenment. To judge claims made in a source in light of one's own values and beliefs, Betti intimates, is a form of disrespect, a refusal to try to understand the source on its own terms and to listen to what it has to say. It is to presume one's own superiority, in cognitive insight, moral judgment, or civilizational attainment, over those whose thought is expressed in the object of interpretation. To criticize Gadamer in these terms seems rather beside the point, given that the latter, as we have seen, rejects the view that the interpreter has access to tradition-independent standards of judgment. Gadamer is concerned to vindicate the authority of tradition, and emphasizes the idea that we must, if understanding is to be possible, be willing to revise our own prejudices as a result of the hermeneutical encounter with the past. To aim for detachment from the source's claim, Gadamer argues, is precisely not to respect its claim to truth, but to disregard it.

The crux of the debate between Betti and Gadamer, then, is whether Gadamer is right to argue that his *Vorgriff* is a condition of the very possibility of understanding, of the ability to interpret a source, to assign meaning to it. This question cannot be discussed here *in extenso*. Some brief remarks on Betti's theory of meaning, however, are nevertheless in order. Betti's theory of meaning, as it is presented in the text published here, employs an expressive model.[21] An expressive model of meaning assumes that the meaning or semantic content of externally observable representative forms derives from the semantic content of the thoughts in the mind of the producer which they are intended to express. Thoughts, in turn, as inner events, are originally meaningful or intrinsically representational, they carry semantic content even if they are not expressed. For Betti, the correctness of hermeneutic understanding, as we have seen, hinges on whether the interpreter succeeds in reconstructing the content of the thought the producer of a signifier intended to express. All that is required in order to interpret successfully, Betti might well have replied to Gadamer, on the basis of this theory of meaning, is for the interpreter to find out what that thought was, and not to judge whether it is true or well-warranted. The claim that this pairing of inner thought with observable representative form is possible only if we presume that all or most of the thoughts whose expressions we are trying to understand are true seems mysterious and unmotivated. We are perfectly capable, after all, to understand false thoughts as well as true.

---

21 See Betti, *Hermeneutik als allgemeine Methode* (n. 1), pp. 7–13 [pp. 4–13].

A Gadamerian is likely to point out, in reply, that Gadamer's *Vorgriff* has been vindicated by arguments put forward in analytical philosophies of language and meaning, which have increasingly come to emphasize the public and social character of meaning and to reject the view that inner mental states can be regarded as intrinsically meaningful. One development of this theme that is particularly congenial to Gadamer's hermeneutical claims, at least at first glance, is Donald Davidson's theory of radical interpretation.[22]

Davidson asks how it would be possible for us to translate or to interpret the utterances of speakers of a language that is, initially, altogether unknown to us. The only data that we could appeal to so as to develop and test hypotheses concerning the meaning of sentences of the unknown language is the observable linguistic behaviour of its speakers. We might, for instance, observe that speakers of the unknown language tend to utter the words 'Yağmur yağıyor!' when it is raining, and come to conjecture that they are to be translated as 'It is raining!'. In doing so, however, we must make a number of assumptions that cannot be falsifiable if the project of interpretation or translation is ever to get off the ground. We must assume, for instance, that speakers of the unknown language, when they utter the words 'Yağmur yağıyor!', aim to describe their surroundings, the situation they are in fact in, and that they are making a statement about it which they hold to be true. What is more, we must assume that the utterance they make is indeed true, for we would otherwise be unable to treat it as a description of the state of affairs that we concomitantly observe to obtain, i.e., that it is raining. Radical interpretation, Davidson concludes, must be committed to a principle of charity. If we are to be able to interpret an unknown language, we must assume that what speakers of that language say is by and large true. Disagreement or the attribution of mistake are possible only against a background of agreement.[23]

It might appear, then, that Betti's hermeneutics is little more than a historical curiosity, a belated attempt to defend the romantic tradition in hermeneutics, associated with Schleiermacher and Dilthey, which rests on an unsustainable theory of meaning. What I would like to suggest by way of conclusion is that it would be grave mistake, despite its philosophical deficiencies, to discard Betti's hermeneutics and to score the debate a victory

---

22 See Donald Davidson, *Inquiries into Truth and Interpretation* (Oxford: Clarendon Press, 1984).

23 Davidson, ibid., p. 137 puts the point as follows: 'If we cannot find a way to interpret the utterances and other behaviour of a creature as revealing a set of beliefs largely consistent and true by our own standards, we have no reason to count that creature as rational, as having beliefs, or as saying anything.'

for Gadamer. Betti's four canons encapsulate an understanding of the real challenge of understanding that is in some important respects more productive than Gadamer's.

To see why this is the case, we need to note that Gadamer's adaptation of what he takes to be the juristic model of hermeneutics is subtly ambiguous. Gadamer's key claim is that the acknowledgment of the authority of tradition, of the truth of its claims, is a precondition of understanding. On one reading of this claim, Gadamer is putting forward a purely descriptive thesis. It is a fact that we do understand each other, and the challenge that Gadamer's hermeneutics intends to meet is that of explaining how this understanding is possible.[24] The answer that Gadamer gives to the question is similar, in broad outline, to Davidson's. When we understand or interpret, we apply a principle of charity, whether we are aware of it or not. We assume, unless there are specific reasons to think otherwise, reasons that presuppose successful interpretation, that what speakers (or authors of historical sources) tell us is true. Disagreement can at best be local.

The problem with reading Gadamer along these lines is that the reading does not sustain his apparent normative claim that tradition has an authority to which we ought to be willing to defer, in cases where the claims of authority stick in our craw. A claim to authority, attributed to tradition, could become relevant only in situations where we, as implicit addressees of the claims of the tradition to which we are held to belong, understand what the tradition claims but fail to be convinced by the claim or even disagree with it. It may well be true that such disagreement could only occur against a backdrop of far-reaching agreement with the beliefs embedded in tradition. When it occurs, however, it cannot be overcome by appeal to the conditions of the possibility of understanding. The very fact that we disagree, and understand what we disagree about, shows that the precondition of agreement that makes understanding possible has already been satisfied.

Perhaps Gadamer wants to claim no more than that it might turn out, when we meaningfully disagree with the claims of tradition, that the claims of tradition are true while ours are false, but this observation, while undoubtedly true, is rather banal and does nothing to show that we have reason to attribute epistemic or practical authority to tradition. It seems clear that Gadamer is interested in raising a stronger normative demand on behalf of tradition. Claims of tradition, or so Gadamer suggests in his discussion of 'the classical', are to be granted a presumption of truth or bindingness, even in the face of what seems to be meaningful disagreement, if they have survived a long series of hermeneutical encounters or re-appropriations

---

24 Compare Betti, *Hermeneutik als allgemeine Methode* (n. 1), p. 51, n. 118 [p. 60, n. 4].

without having lost their hold on us.[25] This suggestion strikes me as deeply problematic. It appears to imagine that the recurring hermeneutic re-appropriations of tradition that have turned out to preserve the authority of its claim(s) have all taken place in the context of a freewheeling Habermasian dialogue, one that gave equal recognition to the claims of all participants and the outcomes of which turned on nothing other than the forceless force of the better argument. The point that the traditions to which we may be taken to belong have not usually been maintained in this way needs no further elaboration.

Gadamer's understanding of juristic hermeneutics, what is more, unduly mystifies the authority of law. Many legal theorists, to be sure, argue that law possesses practical authority, or at least that it necessarily claims such authority, but this authority is commonly explained by appeal to what I have above called the 'settlement-function' of positive law, not by appeal to the view that law, since it purports to be binding, must be presumed to communicate practical truth. We clearly can understand what a law requires of us, and even recognize its bindingness, without having to believe that those who made it were possessed of privileged moral insight. The proper practical attitude towards law, or at least towards law that indeed serves a socially useful settlement-function, is 'to obey punctually; to censure freely',[26] not to defer unquestioningly.

I pointed out above that Betti resists the imposition of meaning onto a source, at least in part, for what appear to be moral reasons. To impose meaning is to disrespect the source, to refuse to understand it on its own terms and to listen to what it has to say. We have seen that this charge does not really apply to Gadamer's hermeneutics, which aims to vindicate the authority of tradition. If anything, Gadamer goes too far in his demand for respect for the claims we might encounter in tradition. One can listen, at least once there is enough background-agreement for understanding to be possible, which is the case wherever we can meaningfully disagree, without attributing authority to the claims one finds expressed in an object of interpretation.

The mixture of detachment and sympathetic engagement that the canons of Betti's hermeneutics demand of the interpreter may well point towards a more productive way to deal with hermeneutical encounters of this kind. A claim we find puzzling, that sticks in our craw, though we believe we understand it, calls for a more conscious hermeneutical effort than is involved in ordinary understanding, one that brackets both the

---

25 See Gadamer, *Truth and Method* (n. 14), pp. 286–291.
26 Jeremy Bentham, *A Fragment on Government*, ed. by F.C. Montague (Oxford: Clarendon Press, 1891), p. 101.

claims of tradition and, as far as possible, our own prejudices. What such bracketing promises, and what good history delivers, is an experience of profound difference that nevertheless remains intelligible. It also provides us with a sensibility to the fact that historical processes, including the ones that have formed our present, were often driven by power and violence as opposed to suasion. What nevertheless permits us to understand other cultures or historical epochs is our shared humanity, not the fact, as Gadamer would have it, that we and the object of interpretation are already enclosed within the same horizon, within a particular tradition which constitutes our own historical existence and lays rightful claim to our allegiance. The hermeneutical tradition for which Betti spoke may need to be rethought as far as its philosophical basis is concerned, but its emancipatory potential should not be abandoned lightly.

Editorial Preface
Giorgio A. Pinton

The hermeneutics as the general methodology of the sciences of the spirit, that is, *Die Hermeneutik als allgemeine Methodik der Geisteswissenschaften zugleich ein Beitrag zum Unterschied zwischen Auslegung und Sinngebung*, was published by Betti in Germany by J.C.B. Mohr (Paul Siebeck), Tübingen, in 1962 – two years after the publication by the same publisher of *Wahrheit und Methode. Grundzüge einer philosophischen Hermeneutik* by Hans Georg Gadamer – in order to present to the German public in a convenient manner the principal concepts of his own masterpiece, the *Teoria Generale della Interpretazione*, which had been published by *Istituto di Teoria della Interpretazione presso le Università di Roma e di Camerino* in two volumes, with Dott. A. Giuffrè Editore, Milan, in 1955.

In the work of 1962 Betti lamented that his previous monumental work did not generate in Germany but a modest echo and a few reviews, and thus dedicated himself to translate it immediately into German in one volume as the *Allgemeine Auslegungslehre als Methodik der Geisteswissenschaften*, again published in Germany by J.C.B. Mohr (Paul Siebeck), Tübingen, in 1967. This edition is not a strict translation of the original Italian text: Betti made significant and specific changes for the German readers. A second edition of the original Italian text, still in two volumes, corrected and amplified by Giuliano Crifò, a disciple of Betti, was made in 1990 by the same publisher of Milan.

Chronologically, however, we should mention that in 1954, Betti had exposed his most personal conceptions on hermeneutics, which had already matured in a continuous reflection on the topic for more than ten years, in the famous 'Hermeneutisches Manifest', the article titled 'Zur Grundlegung einer allgemeinen Auslegungslehre', that was included in the *Festschrift für Ernst Rabel*, II, 1954, pp. 79–168, and in which Betti mentioned and commented on the main topics of the theory. It is important to mention that in 1968, the general theory of interpretation was the topic of study of the specific Convention in Salzburg with the title 'Hermeneutik als Weg heutiger Wissenschaft', of an interdisciplinary character and it was at that time that Emilio Betti was mentioned, together with Friedrich Schleiermacher and Wilhelm Dilthey, as being considered and classified among the most significant and classic representative scholars of hermeneutics (for this see Norbert Henrichs, *Kleine Bibliographie der Hermeneutik und ihrer Anwendungsbereiche seit Schleiermacher*, Düsseldorf: Philosophia-Verl., 1968).

The present translation of the treatise *Die Hermeneutik als allgemeine Methodik der Geisteswissenschaften* comes from the review of the second edition of the work made by the author and published posthumously by Mohr, Tübingen, in 1972.

The integral translation of this work corrects the lacunas of some translations for the most dispersed through Italian journals or in various published works, and makes known the terminology, especially used in the *Teoria Generale della Interpretazione*, that Betti has adopted for the publication and translation of his works in the German language.

1 Hermeneutical problematics in contemporary consciousness

Hermeneutics, as the wide-ranging problematics of interpretation, emerged with such a wealth of motives during the splendid epoch of the European spirit that was called Romanticism. During that cultural period, hermeneutics was the object of the common intent of the experts in the sciences of the spirit—the linguists like Wilhelm von Humboldt and the theologians like Friedrich Schleiermacher; the historians of literature and philologists like F. Ast, August Wilhelm Schlegel and August Boeckh; jurists like Friedrich Karl von Savigny; historians of politics like Reinhold Niebuhr and after him Leopold von Ranke, and then again Johann Gustav Droysen. The venerable hermeneutics (in the sense of a theory of interpretation), in Germany, no longer is an ideal and an active patrimony in the ambience of the sciences of the spirit. Today, with some significant exceptions, it seems that the rich patrimony of hermeneutical thought has been forgotten in its many perspectives, and that the continuity with the great Romantic tradition has been broken, though it is difficult to specify up to what degree.

The Conference of 28 January 1959 by Prof. Helmut Coing at Düsseldorf within the "Arbeitsgemeinschaft für Forschung Nordrhein-Westfalen" discussed "The methods of the juridical interpretation and the theories of general hermeneutics" in a gathering of colleagues of which only one half was made of jurists. Coing was manifestly expressing to his compatriots his own regret that today there is a lack of consciousness for the hermeneutical problematics. It is a lamentable fact, considering that in recent times the hermeneutical problematics has been decisively promoted precisely by German thinkers such as Wilhelm Dilthey and Georg Simmel, whose contributions received the praises of the philosopher Robin George Collingwood, the sociologist Raymond Claude Ferdinand Aron, and the historian Henri-Irénée Marrou.

2 Hermeneutical problematics

It appears entirely characteristic, on that occasion, the cautious attitude showed by the speaker (Prof. Coing) in using references to literature which was mostly vague and unable to offer to auditors a precise images.[1]

---

1 The Author is here limiting himself to a kind of vulgarization that begins with the juridical methods of interpretation (distinguishing among them the systematic and historical interpretation, the sociological-ethical). Then, he delineates, with references to Schleiermacher, the "canons" of the modern general theory of interpretation intended as the basic method of the sciences of the spirit—and here he presents the hermeneutic proceeding of the technical hermeneutical interpretation in accordance with Schleiermacher—as an implied "fourth canon" that should make possible the comprehension of "the surplus of meaning of a product of the human spirit" (a concept that derives from Humboldt, and not from Schleiermacher). He returns thus to jurisprudence trying at the same time to justify his position and to show what the above general points of view on hermeneutics can tell us about the problem of interpretation in the juridical field and what influence they, consciously or unconsciously, have done exercises on jurisprudence as science of the spirit to which is applied the interpretation. Facing the reality of the not perspicuous contribution by the side of Coing, contribution that had no reference to literature and did not enlighten the reader about the weight of the different individual impacts, we sensed the duty to clarify for the German reader our own action and intervention. First of all, our inaugural lecture of 15 May 1948 should have been cited; in it, we have traced the lines of a general hermeneutics as a common methodology of the sciences of the spirit, in their complex. The prolusion has been a design that was presenting the principal results of an attempt that started a year before (February 1947) with the intent of a general theory of the interpretation as problematics, epistemology, and method, which were asking for orientations and differentiated applications for the single sciences of the spirit. Among the authors and the sources of knowledge of the problematics we had mentioned, at that time, the greatest thinkers of the German Romanticism and some of their epigones familiar to us from long time before: Friederich Schleiermacher, Wilhelm von Humboldt, H. Steinthal, M. Lazarus, A. Boeckh, W. Dilthey, G. Simmel, Th. Litt, Joachim Wach, and N. Hartmann. In single conferences given in German, from 1950 to 1955, we have searched to illustrate particular aspects and points of view of the theory of interpretation that in our mind was prospectively forming itself: the integrative development of the law, as a part of the task of the interpretation of law; jurisprudence and legal history of law coming to face the problem of interpretation; problems of translation and of the reproductive interpretation; interpretation as general methodology of the sciences of the spirit.

In 1954, our prolusion was published as a part of the *Festschrift für E. Rabel* in a redaction, in German, much amplified with reference to the pertinent literature, to the extent to be considered as a *Hermeneutical Manifesto* for the foundation of a general theory of interpretation.

In 1955, after eight years of assiduous reflection and meditation, the book *Teoria generale della interpretazione* was published. The conferences that preceded it and especially the *Manifest* recently printed should have had given to the German readers the possibility of access to the book and of reawakening their interest: but it was a failed expectation, because of the insufficient awareness of those scripts. In the same 1955, the "Institute for the Theory of Interpretation"—which for several years already had functioned as study center, with the goal of dealing with law hermeneutics (as well as of the general hermeneutics) and as the organ of connectivity between comparative law, legal history, intertemporal and international private law [especially with the aim of investigating the law systems of foreign countries] and the rapports between various juridical orders—Swas juridically recognized.

Further contributions came in 1957 with a lecture on the fundamental problems of the private international rights and with another lecture in 1958 on the modern dogmatics in the history of rights and culture that discussed whether the use of modern juridical dogmatics is justifiable when used in a historical-juridical interpretation.

It is not our intention now to justify the method of the interpretation before a panel of experts, who have doubts about it, but uniquely to delineate the idea of a general methodology of the sciences of the spirit and to offer in addition a contribution on the distinction between "interpretation" and "attribution of meaning" in order to protect recent contestations of the objectivity of results of the interpretative proceeding.

2 Objectivations of the spirit

There is nothing more important and dearer to human beings than understanding each other. No appeal to their intelligence is as attractive as that which comes from traces already disappeared that return to light and speak to it. Anywhere we come into the presence of sensible forms[1] through which another human spirit speaks to our spirit, our interpretive faculty springs up to action in order to find out the meaning of these forms. Everything – from the fugitive spoken word to the silent document and the mute archeological residue; from a piece of writing or a cypher and artistic symbol; from an articulated language to a figurative or musical expression; from an ordinary declaration to personal comportment; from our face's expressions to the forms of our conduct and character[2] – all that comes to the attention of our spirit from that of *another* spirit calls upon our sensibility and intelligence to be understood.[3] We should certainly not confuse among them all the diverse levels in which the multiplicity of the objectivations of the spirit presents themselves to us. We must clearly distinguish the language and the meanings from the sounds that incarnate and the signs that fix them. We must be careful, in general, not to confuse the material support – which, anyway, momentarily or permanently objectified, pertains to the dimension of the physical world – with the significant content consigned to it, given as to an instrument of the process that in a certain manner implicates it. The thought contained has a meaning that is collocated at a level from the physical that is radically different.[4]

---

1 Cf. "Hermeneutisches Manifest" in *Festschrift Rabel,* II vol. 1954, "Zur Grundlegung einer allgemeinen Auslegungslehre" (For the foundation of a general theory of interpretation), note 1.
2 *Ibid.*, note 2.
3 *Ibid.*, note 3.
4 *Ibid.*, note 4.

3 Representative forms

We must definitively accept that an interpretation can be only actually performed in the actual presence of a representative form – this kind of "form" must be understood in its widest sense. Each form is, in fact, a unitary correlative structure in which a series of perceivable elements are in a reciprocal rapport; a structure, that is, capable of preserving the imprints of its creator or of whatever is embodied in it. The representative function that is essentially needed by such form in order to communicate some knowledge does not need to be necessarily a conscious function. Its significant content is recognizable through the representative function proper of the form, in the sense that through it another spirit, intimately similar to ours, would speak to us, sending a stimulating signal to our own sensitivity and intelligence.[1] Through the representative forms alone that affect an active perception or are reawakened in memory as images of remembrances, a human being is given the possibility of establishing a spiritual commonality with other human beings.[2]

It would be a fall into a rough materialistic prejudice, however, to conceive the "forms," especially the declarative ones, as some kind of envelopes which are exchanged to transmit thought that is wrapped in them.[3] In reality, human beings do not succeed in reaching a reciprocal understanding through material signs of things and do not even succeed in trying to place themselves in the condition of generating the same thoughts through an automatism of transmission, but do so only in so far as each of them causes in the other the same ring in the chain of its own ideas and notions. At this point, in each one, in its spiritual instrumentality the same chord is touched to cause the ideas that correspond to the ones of the other person who is

---

1 Cf. "Hermeneutisches Manifest" in *Festschrift Rabel*, II vol. 1954, "Zur Grundlegung einer allgemeinen Auslegungslehre", note 5a.
2 *Ibid.*, note 5b.
3 *Ibid.*, note 6.

speaking.[4] The doors of our mind can be opened only from the inside and by a spontaneous impulse: what one receives from the exterior is simply the stimulation to vibrate interiorly in harmony with the impulse and to find an accord in commonality.

4 *Ibid.*, note 7a.

4 Representative function & expressive value

The interpretation does not by necessity presuppose that thought must be expressed consciously with a representative practical goal or with an intention of individual communication, due to the social life. Even an activity of thought void of such interest and comportment, which are not directly to be expressive of thought, can be an object of interpretation, in so far as it is an activity whose expressive value makes itself recognizable, in such a way that is possible to obtain from it a style of creativity or a life-style.[1] Every practical individual comportment has its own implicit representative value, sometimes unconscious, but nonetheless symptomatic, which becomes relevant in situations in which one must reflectively value and develop that specific action as an indication that lets transpire the mentality of the personality of the one who acted or is acting, and its particular mode of seeing and judging. It is certainly difficult to succeed in the formulation of such kind of illation on the basis of a single action, when there is no knowledge of possible precedent and subsequent circumstances, which with it would form some kind of rings as in a chain. In a contrary situation, if the circumstances are known, a reference to the personality, in its complexity, may become possible.

In the jurist as well as in the historian, their personal interest for this is born from the fact that the practical comportments, because of their identical essence of being a representative finality, are the most genuine and sincere indications that reveal the orientation of a subject, allowing a secure *illation* about the mode of thinking of the one individual who in that manner comported itself. This concern is awakened in the historian in view of its task of reaching – beginning from the line of the practical conduct effectively implied in an act – the right manner of valuing the possible interplaying interests. The honest focusing on such valuation may be

---

1 Cf. "Hermeneutisches Manifest" in *Festschrift Rabel*, II vol. 1954, "Zur Grundlegung einer allgemeinen Auslegungslehre", note 9.

compromised by some sublimation due to interferences of moralizing tendencies, or to obstacles made by an interest in not permitting the clarification of the actual motivations. It is important to know that even in the cases just mentioned, the object of interpretation remains always the objective realization of a thought that makes itself recognizable in a practical bearing.[2] The reason is that the attitude shown in it must be valued as the one that presents indirectly or implicitly a given mode of seeing or thinking. And this, considered in its value of being an indication, can qualify itself as a representative form, in the wide sense of being an objectification of the human spirit. In the hermeneutical field, we face here the distinction that refers to the essential characters of the representing function proper of the significant forms; a distinction that is justifiable either in the case that the function is immediate, explicit, and consciously developed, or in the case that could be indirect, implicit, and undeveloped. For this reason, in the field of historical materials, the sources of the information transmitted by the written tradition, oral or figurative, are distinguished from the surviving residues, vestiges, or rudiments that emerged as fragments of the past times. The latter ones are characterized by the absence of a conscious representative function, and, in addition, by the rapport that they have as fragments to the whole of the past epoch.

---

2 *Ibid.*, note 10b.

5 To interpret and to understand

In my way of thinking, the interpretive process is destined overall to resolve the epistemological problem of the understanding. By applying the well-known distinction between action and event, process and result, we may provisionally define the *interpretation* as a process whose object and adequate result is the *understanding*. To interpret, from the point of view of its task, signifies "to bring one to understand something." In order to grasp the unity of the interpretive process, one must consider the elementary phenomenon of understanding, as it is actualized by way of language.[1] This phenomenon – illustrated with insuperable clarity by Wilhelm von Humboldt[2] – shows that we should not conceive the language used by others as a material object already fully completed, which we can make ours as any material object or as anything else that is corporeal, but as the plastic source of an incitement addressed to our intelligence, so that we would retranslate what has been perceived, reconstructing from within ourselves its signification, re-expressing with our mental categories the ideas raised up by the line of thought and by the words that have been addressed to us by someone other, in a shaping process that would give them a form.[3]

---

1 Cf. "Hermeneutisches Manifest" in *Festschrift Rabel*, II vol. 1954, "Zur Grundlegung einer allgemeinen Auslegungslehre", note 14b.
2 *Ibid.*, note 15.
3 *Ibid.*, note 15a.

6   The act of interpretation as a triadic process

The observations of W. von Humboldt can manifestly be generalized. The interpretive process, used and intended for resolving the problem of understanding, is unique and always equal in its essential stages, no matter how necessary the differentiation of its applications.

It is always a question of an exigency that solicits the spiritual spontaneity of one person that is called upon to understand; it is an exigency that without the latter's collaboration[1] cannot obtain its effect. It is, truly, an invitation and an exigency that both begin from *representative forms*, within which a certain spirit has been objectified, and reaches a different living and thinking spirit, which is stimulated and moved to understand what is happening by some interests in its present life that can be differently orientated. This phenomenon, therefore, presents itself as a *triadic* process, and its extremes are, on one side, the interpreter, which is a living and thinking spirit, and on the other side, the spirit that has been objectified in the representative forms. These extremes do not come precisely into contact and are not aware immediately of each other, but only as soon as they go through the mediation of those forms in which the objectified spirit faces the interpreter and shows itself as being *some other reality*, as an irremovable objectivity. Subject and object of the interpretational process – that is, the one that interprets and the representative forms – are the same two entities that can be found in every act of understanding.[2] In this case, be aware, that the subject and object appear characterized by some specific qualifications that are determined by the fact that this object is not like any other object but precisely an objectification of a spirit, and the task of the learning subject consists in returning to acknowledge in the objectivations the specific creative thought that animates them, in rethinking their conceptions, or in

---

1 Cf. "Hermeneutisches Manifest" in *Festschrift Rabel*, II vol. 1954, "Zur Grundlegung einer allgemeinen Auslegungslehre", note 16.
2 *Ibid.*, note 16a.

re-evoking the intuition that in them is revealed.[3] To understand is, then, a *re*-cognition and a *re*-construction of a meaning and with the meaning a recognizable spirit through the representative forms of its objectifications and that speaks to the learning spirit, which[4] feels itself similar to it in the commonality of human nature.[5] It is a kind of coming together through a bridge, a joining and a connecting of those forms to the interior totality that produced them and from which they have been removed by a process of interiorization, transposing their own content into another subjectivity, different from the original one.[6]

---

3 *Ibid.*, note 17.
4 *Ibid.*, note 17a.
5 *Ibid.*, note 17b.
6 *Ibid.*, note 18.

7 Inversion of the creative process and transposition into one another subjectivity

What has been said in the last above sentence expressed an *inversion* of the creative process, an inversion through which the interpreter in its hermeneutical path (*iter hermeneuticum*, interpretive mode) must back over, in a retrospective way, the genetic route (*iter geneticum*, creative mode), rethinking it in its own inner being.[1]

The difficulty of this kind of inversion consists of the mentioned *transposition* into another subjectivity, different from the original one. From this, an antinomy is derived between two contrasting exigencies to which the interpretation must bring an equal solution. On one side, the exigency of *objectivity* is challenging the interpreter, in so far as the reproduction of the meaning of the representative forms must correspond, in the most faithfully possible way, to their significant content; thus, this is an exigency of genuine subordination. On the other side, the exigency of objectivity is realizable only through the *subjectivity* of the interpreter, through its capacity of becoming conscious of the conditioning from which the possibility of an adequate understanding of the object depends. All this is like saying that the interpreting individuum is called to reproduce the patrimony of thought of another person and to recreate that thought from his own interiority as something of its own, and, nonetheless, once it has become its own, he still must present it to itself as something objective and as the patrimony of some other person than itself.[2] Thus, we have the antithesis of, on the one hand, the subjectivity that is inseparable from the spontaneity of the understanding, and, on the other hand, the objectivity, that is, the extraneity of the meaning to be discovered. Later on, we will see how all the dialectics of the interpretive process originates from this *antinomy*, and how it is possible to construct

---

1 Cf. "Hermeneutisches Manifest" in *Festschrift Rabel*, II vol. 1954, "Zur Grundlegung einer allgemeinen Auslegungslehre", note 19.
2 *Ibid.*, note 20.

on it a general theory of interpretation. In an identical fashion, we will know that the dialectics of every cognitive process develops from the antinomy between the actuality of the subject and the alterity of the object.

8 The directives of interpretation
The canon of the hermeneutical autonomy of the object

Of all the criteria and the canons that must be followed and that we could call hermeneutic *canons*, some refer to the object and others to the subject of the art of interpretation.

Concerning the canons relative to the object, the *first* fundamental canon is of an immediate evidence. Therefore, if the representative forms that are the object of the interpretation are, by their nature, objectivations of a single spirituality and, specifically, are manifestations of thought, then it is evident that they must be understood according to the otherness of a different active spirit that has objectified itself in them. Manifestly, these representative forms should not be understood according to a spirit and a thought from a different agent, and not even according to a meaning that could be attributed to a nude form by itself, if in considering it, we could disregard the representative function that serves to the given spirit and given thought. In the past few centuries, the theoreticians of hermeneutics incisively formulated this canon of the *mens dicentis*: "Sensus non est inferendus, sed efferendus": meaning should not be assigned unduly and surreptitiously to representative forms, but, on the contrary, must be deduced from them.

I would propose to call this first canon, canon of the hermeneutic *autonomy* of the object, or canon of the immanence of the hermeneutic criterion. With this we mean that the representative forms must be understood in their autonomy, in the way of their own law of formation, in the context into which they will be involved, and according to their inner necessity, coherence, and rationality. The representative forms must, thus, be appreciated in the immanent manner in which they were originally determined; considered as works, they must correspond to their original determination—from the point of view of the author (we can say, demiurge) and for the formative intention at the act of their genesis;

they should not, because of their adaptability, serve to this or that extrinsic scope that would seem most obvious to the interpreter.[1]

---

1 Cf. "Hermeneutisches Manifest" in *Festschrift Rabel*, II vol. 1954, "Zur Grundlegung einer allgemeinen Auslegungslehre", note 24.

9 The canon of the coherence of meanings (The principle of totality)

A *second* fundamental canon that relates to the object to be interpreted is placed in evidence by the Roman Jurist Publius Juventius Celsus in a famous text, of which the polemic point is against the atomizing quibbles of the perorations of the rhetoricians. The hermeneutic canon expressed in the text could be qualified as the canon of *totality* and coherence of the hermeneutic consideration. This canon clarifies the reciprocal rapport and the actual coherence inherent in the various constitutive parts of the discourse – as it happens, in general, any time when a thought is shared – and the common reference to the whole of which they are the parts. Correlations and references make possible a reciprocal illumination and a transparency of the meanings in the representative forms so that the comparison is available of the totality with its own parts and of the parts with the totality.[1]

The correlation between the parts and the totality, that is, their synthesis and their internal coherence, will respond to a requirement of our spirit – an exigency common to the author and to the interpreter – and can be said to be admitted also by the public common sense. If we look at the Romantic hermeneutics, we find that this necessity of a totality is affirmed with particular insistence and energy by Schleiermacher. He manifested his thought by focusing on the circle of the hermeneutical reciprocity that runs between the unity of the totality and the single elements in a work. This reciprocity, he stated, would consent to embark on the interpretation of the work, either by reaching the understanding of the unity and oneness of the totality through its single parts, or by reaching the understanding of the meaning of the single parts in function of the unity of the totality. It is here presumed, then, that the totality of the discourse, like that of any other

---

1 Cf. "Hermeneutisches Manifest" in *Festschrift Rabel*, II vol. 1954, "Zur Grundlegung einer allgemeinen Auslegungslehre", note 27. In addition, *see* E. Betti, *Teoria generale della Interpretazione* (Volume I, 1955), ch. 3, especially pp. 304 ff., §§ 15-20a. Cf. Emilio Betti, *General Theory of Interpretation*, Made in USA (2015), Vol. 2, chs. 2-3, §§ 15-20a.

manifestation of thought, is generated by a unique spirit and is tending to a unique spirit and meaning.[2] Now, from the basis of the manifested correspondence between the *iter geneticum* and the *iter hermeneuticum,* the criterion is derived of extracting from the single elements the meaning of the totality and of understanding each single element in function of the totality of which it is an integrative part. In the same way that the signification, the intensity, and the shadows of a word cannot be intended in any other manner than in the context in which the word was expressed, thus also the meaning and the value of a proposition, and of those connected with it, cannot be comprehended in any other way than from the reciprocal nexus, from the significant concatenation, and from the organic complex of the discourse in which they are found as segments.[3]

The criterion of the reciprocal illumination of the parts and the totality can be farther developed if we could observe how every discourse and each script could be considered at its own turn as a ring in a chain, fully comprehensible only at the light of a more per se comprehensive concatenation. The complex totality in which the single segment must integrate itself should be seen, as in Schleiermacher,[4] with a subjective personal reference to the life of the author, as to its entire life; none of its acts connected to the complex of the others in the measure of the reciprocal influence and illumination, should be understood otherwise than as a moment tied to all the other moments of life of an entire personality. The complex totality, however, can be comprehended also by objectively referring it to a cultural system within which the work is to be interpreted, in so far as it constitutes a ring in the concatenation of meanings existing among the works of a consimilar kind and content. Thus, we must say, the comprehension, at this superior level, will still have, at the beginning of the interpretive process, a provisory character that will progressively consolidate and enrich itself.[5]

In the field of jurisprudence, the hermeneutical canon of totality is applied to the interpretation of the declarations and comportments both of juridical norms and precepts as well as of maxims of decisions. The field of its application is, nonetheless, much wider. The penal treatment of a delinquent, according to the postulate of the positive school of penal rights, requires that one should move from the single criminal action considered in its own symptomatic value, to the consideration of the specific individual personality that the author manifested in such conduct.[6] Clearly, this process

---

2 *Ibid.*, note 27a.
3 *Ibid.*, note 28.
4 *Ibid.*, note 30.
5 *Ibid.*, note 31.
6 *Ibid.*, note 32.

respects the exigency of a reference to the totality. Equally we appeal, more or less consciously, at the canon of totality in the interpretation of juridical norms and laws, especially when we aim at excluding interpretations contrary to the logic of the elaborated system with the instruments of the legal dogmatics, of which the norm to be interpreted is an integrative part.[7] An example of this is the need of excluding the application of single maxims of decisions to be extracted (according to the criteria of the international private rights) from foreign juridical decisions, in so far as these decision are foreign, that is, may be in contrast with the spirit of the local proper legal order.[8] Even prescinding from the specific preoccupation which emerges in rapport with the insertion of a maxim of decision that is contrastive with the system, already from the concept of the juridical order elaborated by the modern juridical dogmatics, we can derive the idea that every norm or maxim of decision destined to become an integrant part of that legal system, must have a necessary relation to its totality. Now, that kind of totality – using an expression of Dilthey – constitutes an active concatenation that is productive and that creates an organic correlation, an interdependence, a harmonic coherence and a cohesion also between the norms and the groups of norms in juridical different fields.[9]

---

7 *Ibid.*, note 33.
8 *Ibid.*, note 34. *See* E. Betti, "Grundprobleme des internationalen Privatrechts," in *Jus et Lex,* Festgabe für Max Gutzwiller, 1959, p. 245, note 31.
9 *Ibid.*, note 35.

10 Analogy and integrative development

Moving from the consideration of the object to be interpreted, we will begin to consider the active subject. We find an ulterior criterion in the application of rights and responsibilities by a jurist, as well as by a theologian, when one recognizes as justified the exigency of integrating the interpretation of an imperfect or incomplete discipline or of limiting it in the presence of a juridical-political motive, or it has been decided, on the contrary, to forbid that a juridical prescription, established and accepted against the coherent consequence of a system of law, would constitute a precedent for ulterior conclusions. Here, the problem is not only that of referring a particular case to a totality of a superior order (the totality of the legal order or of the universe of faith), but of integrating the achieved evaluation in its finalistic rationality, obtaining from it an excess of significance that will permit ulterior conclusions in relation to the convivence of the consociated in an identical legal or religious community, or that, on the contrary, will require, for its limited basis, to be applied only in a limited manner. It is evident that the integration or the restriction here required – that in our time are designated as an analogy, an extensive interpretation and a restrictive interpretation – are introducing in the process of interpreting an element that goes beyond the simple task of recognition of meaning, and adds the ulterior task of adaptation and adequacy.[1] This new task completes a function of integration and of application that moves toward a complementary development of the legal norms, and respectively of the directives given to the faithful members, at the inside of the pre-existent social structures, and of bringing them to face accordingly the present actual realities.

In line with the categories of the autonomy of the object and of the hermeneutic totality – which obey in the same way the exigency immanent to the object to be interpreted, considered in its interior coherence and in

---

1 Cf. "Hermeneutisches Manifest" in *Festschrift Rabel*, II vol. 1954, "Zur Grundlegung einer allgemeinen Auslegungslehre", note 39-40.

its concatenations, which both respond to the problem of the objectivity of the meaning to be achieved – an attentive reflection discovers some other canons to be observed in the interpretation. They are canons that obey to the exigency of an efficient collaboration with the individual subject charged with the task of understanding, and they respond thus to the specified moment of the subjectivity inseparable from the spontaneity of the understanding.

11 Canon of the actuality of understanding

There is another canon that primarily should be obeyed in every interpretation. It is the *third* canon that deals with the actuality of the understanding and which Rudolf Bultmann recently has drawn attention to.[1] According to this canon, the interpreter should run through again with its mind, in an inverse way, the genetic process and reconstruct from within itself and resolve within its own proper actuality, the thought of someone else, a piece of the past or the memory of a personal experience; that means to say that the interpreter should absorb it as an event in its own personal experience, thanks to a sort of transposition, within the circle of its own spiritual horizon, in virtue of the same synthesis with which it recognizes and reconstructs it.[2] Precisely for this reason, the aspiration of some historiographers who wish to free themselves of their own subjectivity appears entirely absurd. In the field of historical interpretation it would be naive to think that the task of the historiographer is fully completed in the simple representation of what the sources are testimonies, and to believe that true history is uniquely the one given by the sources.[3] Whoever thinks this way forgets that all what our mind can make its own enters for the simple fact to be part of the organic totality of the world of concepts and representations that we carry already within ourselves. Thus, every new experience becomes, for reasons of a certain assimilation, alive part of our spiritual cosmos, and consequently every time that new experiences are received in that cosmos,[4] they are subjected to its own identical vicissitudes.

---

1 In his book, *Geschichte und Eschatologie* (1958). On the actuality of understanding. Also, Bultmann, *History and Eschatology: The Presence of Eternity*, The Gifford Lectures 1955, Harper Torchbooks, New York & Evanston, 1962, pp. 104-109, 111.
2 "Hermeneutisches Manifest: Zur Grundlegung einer allgemeinen Auslegunslehre," note 41.
3 *Ibid.*, note 43.
4 *Ibid.*, note 44.

12 The vital rapport with the subject-matter & the direction of the inquiry

It is certainly true that the duty of the interpreter is uniquely to research and understand the meaning of a thought expressed by someone else (eventually also in the past),[1] that is, the modes of conceiving and representing that are revealed in such an expression. The meaning and the mode of representation are not able to offer ready representative forms to be grasped by an interpreter who is merely receptive or that could be received or collected with a passive and mechanical operation. Meaning and mode of representation are instead something that the interpreter must recognize and reconstruct within itself, by way of its own sensibility, its own intelligence, and through the categories of its own mind, with the intuition and the inventive powers due to its own learning.[2]

Generally, in our times, we are conscious and concord in recognizing that the attitude of the interpreter should not be passively receptive, but actively reconstructive. However, in underlining these facts, we have gone, in our opinion, too far. That has happened not so much like when it has been postulated in the interpreter a certain "pre-understanding" – which is an ambiguous way to say that the interpreter must possess an understanding of the subject-matter,[3] that is, in a vital rapport with the particular reality[4] that he tries to comprehend. There is no ambiguity in this; the formula, as it is expressed here, should be absolutely innocuous, but has become ambiguous when the question has been raised whether it would be possible to achieve, through an interpretation, an objective knowledge.[5] In order to avoid misunderstandings we must immediately admit that, in the sciences of

---

1 "Hermeneutisches Manifest: Zur Grundlegung einer allgemeinen Auslegunslehre," note 44a.
2 *Ibid.*, note 45.
3 *Ibid.*, note 14a.
4 Bultmann, *Geschichte und Eschatologie* (1958), p. 126; or *History and Eschatology*, p. 113.
5 Thus, recently Bultmann, in *Geschichte und Eschatologie*, pp. 129–137; *History and Eschatology*, pp. 115–122.

the spirit, objectivity has a whole different meaning than in the sciences of nature, in which we are dealing with an object essentially different from us.[6] However, nonetheless, we must decisively refute the inconsiderate consequence that someone has derived from it, that is to say that it is impossible to maintain a clear distinction of the subject who wants to know from the object to know,[7] or that the objectivity of the historical phenomena is nothing more than a phantasm, that is, "the illusion of an objectivizing way of thinking which is truly appropriate in natural science but not in history."[8] The valid argument of Bultmann derives from the thesis that "in the historical knowledge it is not possible to reach objectivity, not even in the sense that the phenomena could be known in their own objectivity, because this objectivity will be the illusion of an objectifying thought."[9] Bultmann presents the argumentation as follows: the conditions of each understanding interpretation is the preceding vital rapport with the subject-matter, directly or indirectly expressed in the text, and that indicates where to direct the inquiry (this is what Bultmann intends with the German *Vorverständnis*: pre-understanding; an ambiguous term, equivocal and to be avoided).[10]

According to Bultmann, the type of question to be proposed, i.e. the goal towards which the investigation is directed, arises from the concrete interest. In that case, the text gives directly the object of the investigation. But the goal may also be determined by an interest in situations that are present in all the possible texts, in which case the text would supply only indirectly that which we should ask.

(1) The goal of a research can, for example, be given by an interest in the reconstruction of the past; it can be given by a psychologic interest that inquires of the texts with questions in mind concerning individual psychology, social or religious, or in a manner of psychology of language, poetry, art, law.

---

6 Erick Frank, in Bultmann, *Geschichte und Eschatologie*, p. 134; *History and Eschatology*, pp. 119–120.
7 *Ibid.*
8 Bultmann, *Geschichte und Eschatologie*, p. 130; *History and Eschatology*, p. 121. For a critique, cf. my lecture in Zürich on 24 February 1960: "Historische Auslegung und eschatologische Sinngebung," recasted in this script. A symptom of the now days explicit reaction to Heidegger's existentialism can be seen in Th. W. Adorno, *Noten zur Literatur* (Suhrkamp, 1958).
9 Bultmann, *Geschichte und Eschatologie*, p. 136; *History and Eschatology*, p. 121.
10 In the essay "Das Problem der Hermeneutik" (1950) (in *Glauben und Verstehen*, II, p. 211, especially pp. 227–230).

(2) The goal of a research can be also motivated by an esthetic interest that places the texts under a structural analysis and examines the interior form of a work of art; this can also be said in relation to a religious interest, or even by remaining in the setting of a stylistic consideration.

(3) The incentive goal can be given by an interest in history, as in "the ambiance of the life in which the human existence evolves."[11]

This would be "the question about the human existence as the mode of being of the Self." The inquiry that focuses especially on the texts of philosophy, religion, and poetry would be always guided by the provisory understanding of the human existence (an existential understanding) "from which are born generally the categories that make possible a query or a quibble" about salvation and meaning of individual existence, about the ethical norms of conduct, or about the communion with similar human beings. The pre-understanding should be verified critically and tested in the act of understanding: that means to question the text, letting the text to challenge us, and listening to its pretensions.

---

11 *Ibid.*, p. 228.

13 Is it possible to achieve the objectivity of the historical phenomena?

Relying on such convictions, Bultmann gave an answer to the query, "Is it possible to reach an objective knowledge of the historical phenomena, that is, is it possible to reach the objectivity of (historical) interpretation?" After all, the interpretation of historical phenomena is certainly not the same as the one that is used in the sciences of nature. The motivation of Bultmann, however, gives way to an equivocation, and, in addition, it will fail a rigorous critical verification. He thinks that the historical phenomena have no existence if there is no historical subject interested in understanding them, because

> the events of the past – according to him – become historical phenomena only when they appear to be significant to a subject that, being within history, is taking its part in history, that is, when they acquire meaning for the one subject who is connected with them in its historical existence.

Bultmann, then, believes that "the historical phenomenon contains its own future, in which the phenomenon alone will show itself as what it is." If, with this expression, he meant to indicate the remote and near-at-hand consequential effects of the historical phenomenon,[1] then it could be accepted; but then it would be an issue totally different from the historical conditioning of the phenomenon through the existence of a subject that is considering it.

Bultmann considers the historical phenomenon, if studied in the line of the scientific understanding, would have a univocal sense, and would not be under the arbitrariness of whatever interpretation, even though each historical phenomenon would offer many aspects, in so far as it is exposed to different kinds of a general questioning: historical-cultural, psychological,

---

1 In the sense of Droysen, *Historik*, p. 89.

sociological, or in other ways of questioning that are born from the historical connection of the interpreter with the phenomenon. Bultmann admits that every query, if the interpretation is conducted in a methodological correct manner, brings up a univocal understanding and an objective knowledge capable of being adequate to the object when the object is framed in a determined perspective. To qualify the formulation of the inquiry as "subjective" because the query must be determined every time by the choice made by the subject, would be insignificant, for the simple fact that every single phenomenon presents different aspects, and requires its meaning to be shown under various perspectives, and that each interpreter comes to formulate its own inquiry to which the phenomenon must give an answer that is properly specific to solely that interpreter.

The pretension, then, that the interpreter must obliterate its own subjectivity is truly absurd. What the interpreter should uniquely silence is its proper personal wishes about the results of the interpretation, because, as with any scientific research, the absence of imposed conditions is obviously needed. Understanding presupposes the greatest vitality of the subject person and the maximal possible development of its individuality. As the interpretation of art and poetry is successful only in those individuals who let themselves be grabbed by poetry and art, so Bultmann believes that the interpretation alone can be considered as "the understanding of the historical phenomena at the highest and definitive level and sense," that will be able to question the text about the possibility of an authentic human existence. Concluding, Bultmann adds, "the most subjective" interpretation is "the most objective," and that means that only the person who is moved by the question about its own existence is capable of hearing what "the text intends to say." In this context, Bultmann refers himself to an observation of Fritz Kaufmann, an observation that seems to say that the monuments of history

> speak to us, from the depth of the reality that generated them, only if we ourselves, thanks to our favorable disposition to experimenting, know the real problematics, the need, the uncertainty, and the risk, all insurmountable, and that constitute the depth and the abyss of our being in the world.[2]

---

2 Bultmann, *Geschichtsphilosophie der Gegenwart*, 1931, p. 41.

14 Function of the sensibility for the values proper of the historian

The value-relating interpretation

After the exposition of the doctrine of Bultmann, we would like to offer a critique. In our opinion, in the entire context there is an identifiable small and little evident equivocation. If we could find it, then it seems to us that all the argumentations would lose their stringent logics. Is there a tie between the phenomenon and the maximal vitality of the subject? Is it possible for us to get co-involved and to be questioning the texts on the possibility of the human existence as a mode of being of the Self? Surely, it can be recognized as a condition of the possibility itself of the historical interpretation. In that case, we should have an exact knowledge of how things are in regard to the historical "reproduction" of the emotional and sociological contents (when there is the possibility that they will become historically relevant). To make an appeal to the "feelings," when they cannot be translated into well-articulated and demonstrable judgments, that is, into an experience conceptually structured, means to refute a scientific verification, and testify uniquely of the psychological genesis of a hypothesis in the mind of the historian. But as long as the feelings remain at the stage of being personally felt values, there is not even the minimal warranty that such feelings would correspond in some ways to those of the real person with which the historian identifies itself.

This explanation (*Deutung*) in this subjective form and on an emotional base represents neither the historical knowledge of real concatenations nor the knowledge through a *value-relating interpretation* that still could be performed. For this, therefore, we will appeal to Max Weber's exposition.[1]

---

1 Concerning Q. Knies and the so-called problem of irrationality, cf. M. Weber, *Gesammelte Aufsätze zur Wissenschaftslehre*, ed. Johannes Winckelmann, 42–145. Tübingen: J.C.B. Mohr [Paul Siebeck]), pp. 119–122, which were utilized in our *Teoria generale della interpretazione* (1st Edition 1955) Vol. I, pp. 276–278 (§ 13a); (2nd Edition 1990) Vol. I, pp. 276–282 (§ 13a). Cf. Emilio Betti, *General Theory of Interpretation*, Vol. 2, Chapter 2, pp. 83–87 (§ 13a).

With the terms "value-relating interpretation," Max Weber means "the explanation" of an object that can be valued aesthetically, morally, and intellectually or from other cultural perspectives, (without becoming an integrant part of a mere genetic historical exposition), but preferably – if historically considered – becomes a "conformation" (*Formung*) of the historic individuality, that is, the investigation of values, which are realized in that object, and of its individual form, in which they are apparent: an operation, therefore, of the philosophy of history, which is effectively "subjectivist" as it admits that the validity of its values cannot by us be understood as a validity of facts empirically ascertained. The value-relating interpretation does not aim at the clarification of what consciously those individuals – who historically participated to the production of the object to be valued – sensed, but what values we can or we must find in that object. In the latter case, the value-relating interpretation proposes for itself the identic goal of a normative approach, dogmatically oriented – aesthetics, ethics, jurisprudence – and is itself evaluative. In the first case, this interpretation operates through a dialectic analysis of the values and ascertains only the possible value relations to the object. Because of this rapport the interpretation fulfills its important function of exiting from its indetermination about what is "that is sensed only through empathy" and arrives at the types of determination of which the knowledge of individual contents of conscience is capable. Contrary to the merely "sensing" and "empathizing oneself with something else," an operation in which the vitality of an included subject is demonstrated, we call "value" precisely that and only that suitable thing that becomes the content of a taken position, of a conveniently articulated "judgment," that is, something addressing itself to us demanding "validity" and requiring an answer in terms of value; something of which the validity is judged in terms of values for us, and thus accepted, refused, or simply judged in their own multiple knots. The exigence of ethical, aesthetic, or juridical values implies always the formulation of a "judgment of value." For our critical considerations it is important to establish one only thing: what makes the object intended through judgments of value to move out of the sphere of mere "empathy," elevating itself at the level of the sphere of knowledge, is uniquely the determinacy of its content. The pretension of sharing a judgment of value on a certain factual datum would have no sense if what is supposed to be a content of judgment would not be understood in an identical manner in those that are its important points. In some way, the relation between the individuality and a possible value signifies always, in a certain measure, the overcoming of a merely intuitive sensing. The historical individuality can very well be only a unity artificially constructed with reference to ways of values, and the "evaluation" is, for the intellectual comprehension, the normal moment of a psychological transfer. The evaluation functions as the maieutic instrument at the service of the noetic comprehension, a moment in transition in the genesis of its knowing, to which the historian should in any case attempt to arrive. Thus, in presenting the indications of Max Weber,[2] we have also shown the limits within which the subjectivist touch of the value-relating interpretation assumes a correct role in the cognitive process of the historian.

---

2 Max Weber, "Knies und das Irrationalitätsproblem," I-II, in *Gesammelte Aufsätze zur Wissenschaftslehre*, pp. 122–125.

15 The answer to the proposed historical question

The arguments on which the subjectivist doctrine of Bultmann rests reveal, if submitted to a verification, their disputability by manifesting themselves as in part not proving and in another part result as being with a surreptitious equivocation. First of all, any individual could certainly admit that a conception of history is conditioned by the perspective of the historian and that every historical phenomenon can be considered from a multiplicity of different points, but from the historicity of the point of view of the historian no possibility exists to deduce any decisive argument against the objectivity of the historical interpretation. The historical judgment, conditioned by interests of the most various kind, is the only *answer* that from time to time the historian is in grade of furnishing to the correspondent spiritual situation and to the "historical question" (of Johann Gustav Droysen) arising out of it. The objective truth can now be glimpsed, within the limits of the perspective adopted at the various times, from any point of observation.[1] The perceived picture, then, would be considered deformed only if we would pretend that the particular perspective used would be the unique one, that is, the only one admissible and justifiable.[2] Concerning the objection made against the objectivity of the historical interpretation in relation to a so-called "existential encounter with history," it must be said that in it a light equivocation exists. This happens when a condition for the possibility of historical knowledge, namely, the necessary noetic interest and the responsible participation of the historian in history entailed by it, is confused with the object of knowledge itself.[3] There is the same light

---

1 Cf. H. G. Gadamer, "Was ist Wahrheit?" in *Zeitwende* 28, 1957, pp. 226 ff.
2 This is admitted in Bultmann, *Geschichte und Eschatologie*, pp. 132–133; *History and Eschatology*, pp. 119 f.
3 In the same sense Gadamer, *Gründzuge einer philosophischen Hermeneutik*, p. 311; *Truth & Method*, Ed. 1975, pp. 290–291. (Here, see also endnote 81). Cf. F. Nietzsche, *Menschliches, Allzumenschliches*, II, p. 223 (tr. it. Umano troppo umano/Human, too much human).

equivocation in confusing the query on the *meaning* of the historical phenomenon in rapport to the remote and the actual effects, with a query fully different, that questions its *significance* in relation to its relevance on the present time, through the turns of the historical epochs and of the historical mutable conceptions of the same phenomenon in the light of our awareness and of our cultural actual evolution.

16 Meaning of a historical phenomenon and its significance in the present

The equivocation between the signaled concepts is evident when it is asserted that the "objectivity of historical knowledge is not attainable in the sense of absolute ultimate knowledge."[1] This assertion is recognized as justifiable, given the fact that the hermeneutical task never ends. However, it has been than added that "nor in the sense that the phenomena could be known in their very 'being in themselves' which the historian could perceive in pure receptivity."

This second affirmation, allied as it is with the first, makes reference to something fully unlike the first in so far as it denies the very objectivity of historical phenomena. And this is evidently too much. Effectively, the task of an interpretation constantly aware of the actuality of the understanding can never be declared definitive nor considered concluded and complete. No interpretation, no matter how much convincing it appears in the moment when it has been elaborated, can be imposed on the future humanity, as if it were the exact ultimate interpretation.[2] The incompleteness of the hermeneutic task implies that the sense in the texts, monuments, and relics of the past should be renewed continuously by life and eternally transformed in its series of revivals. This does not truly exclude that the objectivized content of meaning in representative forms would remain always the objectivation of the creative energy of some *alien* spirit, with which the interpreter must search and find the necessary communication, not according to its own arbitrariness, but in line with controlled criteria. The fact that the spirit of one other person of the past speaks to us – not with its voice, but through space, time, and a material transformed and full with spiritual energy – and makes us able to approach the sense of these different forms of representation that are parts of the human spirit and all originate (let us say it with Husserl) from the identical transcendental subjectivity, and

1 Bultmann, *Geschichte und Eschatologie*, p. 136; *History and Eschatology*, p. 121.
2 "Hermeneutisches Manifest," note 146a.

nevertheless remain a steadfast self-contained Otherness that can confront us, for the reason that here is an alien mind that has objectified itself in such representative forms.[3] In regard to the second mentioned equivocation – that is, the dis-acknowledgment of the difference between "meaning" (*Bedeutung*) of the single historical phenomena and "significance" (*Bedeutsamkeit*) of the identical phenomena for our present time and for our [sense of] responsibility for the future – we must confess that the equivocation is no less evident when someone asserts that "the historical phenomena are not what they are in pure individual isolation, but only in their relation to the future for which they have importance."[4] The future here intended is "the only one future in which a phenomenon manifests itself for what it really is" (an affirmation that could have an acceptable sense in rapport with the consequential proximal effects of the phenomenon[5]), but then we hear the immediate interference that says that the question concerns "what meaning (more accurately, what 'significance') do the historical events of our past have for our present, a present to which is assigned a responsibility for the future?"[6] If this is what is asserted here, then "Only the historian who is excited by his participation in history (and that means – who is open for the historical phenomena through his sense of responsibility for the future), only he will be able to understand history."[7] In this sense "the most subjective interpretation of history is at the same time the most objective." But this is a paradox that we know from the precedent considerations, a paradox that is verily unresolvable.

---

3 Freyer, *Theorie des objektiven Geistes*, III ed., p. 84.
4 Bultmann, *Geschichte und Eschatologie*, pp. 134–135, 137; *History and Eschatology*, pp. 120–125.
5 Droysen, *Historik*, p. 89.
6 Bultmann, *Geschichte und Eschatologie*, p. 135; *History and Eschatology*, p. 121.
7 *Ibid.*, p. 137; *History and Eschatology*, p. 122.

17 Dialog and monolog

For all that has been said recently, someone could truly raise an objection with regard to meaning and significance. Meaning certainly is a value assigned to an historical phenomenon that is not considered in isolation *per se*, but, according to the mentioned hermeneutical canon of totality in interpreting, it deserved it only in a meaningful concatenation of its consequential and remote effects, in the measure in which it is possible to discover them. Properly, the concatenation would be a concatenation of meaning. This meaning is anyway a meaning that, because of the necessary temporal distance separating the phenomenon from the historian, is like something in itself concluded, and that must be primarily rediscovered. If vice versa it is stated that the proper essence of the phenomenon "ultimately it will show itself in its very essence only when history has reached its end,"[1] then we confuse the point of view of the historical interpretation with that of an attribution of an eschatological meaning. In reality, only from the point of view of such an attribution of meaning, the significance for our present time would appear essentially determined by the position of the interpreter. Only to a present time, "a present which is charged with responsibility for our future," it would make sense to address the problem of the present-day significance of the present actualities, and consider such significance as the product of conferring sense-giving values, an attribution conditioned by the position of the observer. Now, if one identifies the definitive meaning of an historical phenomenon (how it really was) that is given and only needs to be found, with its significance for the present and the future of an observer, which is conditioned by meaning-inference, then it can easily be discerned what, in fact, lies at the heart of "the existential encounter with history." The *dialog* that should be established between the historian and the spirit of the past objectified in the sources will here be missing completely and would be altered into a *monolog*, a soliloquy. What is

---

1 Bultmann, *Geschichte und Eschatologie*, p. 135; *History and Eschatology*, pp. 120–121.

missing is an interlocutor of the dialogue, exactly the one that properly should have been present in the texts, as a spirit un-mistakenly alien and distinct, and by the absence of which any process of interpretation would be utterly unimaginable. If the dialog becomes a soliloquy, the interpreter, who should inquire about the sense of the phenomena (representative forms), should let himself be questioned by the texts! Is it, then, still possible to regard such a procedure as an interpretation? For the present, we want only to raise the problem.

18 Historical interpretation and attribution of an eschatological meaning

Given that in our reasoning we have counter opposed interpretation of meaning and conferring or attribution of meaning, and on that contraposition we have based the lever of our criticism, we have felt the obligation then of clarifying the concept of conferring the meaning as it is made in an eschatology, intending to explain the diversity between eschatology and the science of history. The cognitive power of the spirit is actualized both in the interpretation and in the conferring of meaning, but the first process (the interpretation) and the second one (conferring of meaning) relate to different requirements. The spirit confers sense to the whole universal world in general (and this does not happen in the interpretation), but in a manner more pregnant and elevated the spirit confers sense to objects that in the world possess the spirit's same nature. From this point of view, when referred to the world, the attribution of sense is fortuitous, while when referring to human beings it is regarded as planned.[1]

In rapport with the world, the human being is not conscious of conferring the sense that it does confer; and by that neither does it satisfy a moral requirement imposed on it by the world. Contrariwise, the human being, among its fellow citizens, needs to do justice to them, with its sense of values, but not with action, and not even with its manner of thinking, but simply with looking at, participating in, evaluating, staying, as well, sometimes, and lingering. Now, we know that the human being is capable either of submit to the obligations imposed by an internal justice in response to values, or to disregarding them. The bestowing of meaning, more than just here, is essential in men's power, but it depends on their free choice. Thus, the human being perceives, in the appeal that makes it to feel as an incumbent duty the demand to submit to justice, a moral obligation, in relation to which it may respond with a conduct that is faithful or faithless, making it guilty. Concerning material goods, the human can also avoid sinning by disregarding them; however, he surely sins if

---

1 Hartmann, *Das Problem des geistigen Seins*, 1933, pp. 140 ff.

he disregards his neighbors. To fail here is not a simple damage of lost occasions (a damage that results evident if we would reflect with Nietzsche: "The world is brimming with beautiful things but nevertheless poor, very poor in beautiful moments and in the unveiling of those things"[2]). Failing in this case is to make oneself culpable towards our connatural humans who will see themselves as unworthy, segregated, and excluded from the reality of living, the living community of spirits.

How is, then, the situation in relation to an attribution of eschatological meaning? What do we mean by this? This kind of conferring meaning refers to the *Verbum Dei ut viva vox,* the living Word of God.[3] Considering that the *Eschaton* is beyond the time of history, it could seem that the historical course of time may be irrelevant to the attribution of eschatological meaning, but it is not the case.[4]

We are not in the position to give a judgment on eschatological problems, but the point of issue in this case is the needed demarcation of competence between two intellectual activities, one of which is familiar with us, but not the other. Eschatology, however, lays claim on history and thereby endangers its independence and questions the objectivity of its results. How then can one draw a border between eschatology and history? Given that eschatology does not want to be a metaphysical doctrine of an ultra-terrestrial condition beyond time that has for its own object God's influence on the actions of humanity, and given that the human being exists within running time, consequently even the temporal course of the human existence must be absorbed within the domain of eschatology. Thus, time, too, considered as a chronological succession, becomes located within an eschatological horizon. However, how should we understand such postulated polarity, in Bultmann's viewpoint, between presence and transcendence? If we consider it carefully, the course of history, in Bultmann's eschatology, appears to be of only secondary importance. History can never provide the structure on which the eschatological event crystallizes itself; these events occur, rather, within existence, which cannot be determined by referring to history alone. The presence of Christ, the Parousia, is not, in the Protestant view of Bultmann, historically limited, and, for this reason, is not something already previously set in the human essence; it is an encounter that happens in every epoch, from time to time. The eschatological situation is characterized by the problem of deciding whether existence is open to the "Advent" or remains tied to itself. Through the factual stage of being open to the future, existence is no longer vulnerable,

---

2 *Die fröhliche Wissenschaft,* p. 339 (It. tr.: Nietzsche Works: Nietzsche Online, Hunter College) by Giorgio Colli and Mazzino Montinari).
3 G. Ebeling, "Wort Gottes und Hermeneutik" in *ZThK* 56 (1959), p. 224.
4 Joh. Körner, *Eschatologie und Geschichte,* 1957, p. 52.

but responsible and capable of deciding about itself. Faith must give proof of itself in the course of time; it is the courageous anticipation of the future and confers on it a meaning; it is trusting in the fact that, in view of Christ, what is still beyond the struggle is in fact already reality.[5]

For Bultmann, the taking of this position on the eschatology, seen as attributive of meaning, would be absolutely identical to his direct position toward the knowledge of history, because only the historian, who is moved by personal participation in history – being open to the historical phenomena by way of the sense of responsibility for the future – would be at the level (it is said) of comprehending history. Accordingly, the opinion of Bultmann would tell us that there would be a special reciprocal correspondence between the knowledge of history and the knowledge of oneself. This particular correspondence and assimilation is established by Bultmann as follows:[6] the knowledge of oneself would be consciousness of the responsibility for the future, and the act of self-knowledge would in no way be a contemplative attitude, merely theoretical, but rather an act of choice, exactly as the arduous courageous anticipation of the future that stands at the center of the eschatological doctrine. If this is accepted, then the *historicity* of the human existence could become comprehensible in full only if the factual existence of the human being would be understood as a life with responsibility for the future, as a choices-making life.

If so, we should deduce that historicity does not fully reveal its meaning as a natural quality of the human individual, but only as a possibility that is offered to him and that must be chosen and actualized. The human that lives without knowledge of itself and without the conscience of its responsibility, according to this conception, would not be a being that neglects the practice of inferring meaning that is demanded from it as a duty, but rather a being that, abandoning itself to the relativity of the historical conditionings of its domain, would only represent "a human being in history, at a very low level of maturity." Truly, Bultmann concluded in agreement with Collingwood, "Genuine historicity means to live in responsibility and history is a call to historicity." The coherent consequence of these ratiocinations, in regard to our problem, is found in the affirmation that constitutes its most basic motive for it:

> "In this type of understanding, the traditional counter-opposition of subject and included object disappears. It is only by participating and by being itself a historical being that the student can understand history. In this kind of understanding of history, the human being understands

---

5 *Ibid.*, pp. 52ff.
6 Bultmann, *Eschatologie und Geschichte*, p. 162; *History and Eschatology*, pp. 136–137.

itself; the human nature, in fact, is not grasped by way of introspection, but it is uniquely the history that can tell what the humans are, because history goes across the riches of historical creations and reveals the possibility of the human existence".[7]

---

7 Bultmann, *Eschatologie und Geschichte*, p. 139; *History and Eschatology*, p. 132.

19 The threat of denying the objectivity

The above contention that raises the new problematics could bring to the complete abolition of objectivity, and it is what the historians must resolutely oppose. As the result from our observations tells, the subjectivist orientation is based on the confusion of meaning that identifies the hermeneutic process of the historical interpretation as an attribution of meaning connected with an initial situation (as in the case of the eschatological autoconscience) and that causes to confuse one of the conditions of possibility of that process with what is, instead, its object. The result is that the basic canon of the hermeneutic autonomy of the object is completely eliminated from the cognitive process of the historian.

It is exactly in this hermeneutical procedure that the risk of a misunderstanding is accentuated, with a possible opportunity of gathering from the interrogated texts nothing more than what is esteemed meaningful and reasonable by ourselves, but missing, at the same time, the grasping of what is diverse, what is proper to someone else, which eventually is discarded or, within parentheses, is passed as a myth. What has to be objected to, is, however, evident. The texts, in so far as they are given before the "pre-understanding" that assigns meaning, are not given to re-enforce our pre-constituted and pre-conceived idea; we must rather presuppose that the texts have something to tell us that we, by ourselves, do not yet know and that exists independently from our attribution of meaning,[1]

It is here that the problematics and the disputability of a subjective formulation comes up in full light influenced by the contemporary existential philosophy. From it has come the misunderstanding between interpretation and inferring-meaning and the canon's suppression of the autonomy of the

---

1 Cf. K. Löwith, *Heidegger, Denker in dürftiger Zeit,* 1953, p. 83.

object, with the hard consequence that the objectivity of the results of the interpretive process, in all the sciences of the spirit, is doubtful. We are convinced that it is the duty of historians to defend the objectivity and to demonstrate the epistemological conditions of its possibility.

20 Theological hermeneutic and demythologizing of the Kerygma

The misunderstanding mentioned has been brought to light and partially resolved by some corrections Professor Gerhard Ebeling has made recently to the current views about hermeneutics.[1] In order to distinguish the general hermeneutics from a special theological hermeneutics, Ebeling has taken into consideration the special point of view of Bultmann according to which a specific theological formulation of the question is conditioned by the different orientation of the problems that, with particular structures and criteria, incline to an exegetical and dogmatic comprehension of the texts. All this, however, postulates a nexus that is demonstrable with a general theory of understanding. But, how should we formulate the nexus? Or, what is the reciprocal rapport between words and understanding? Or, which one is the substantial constitutive element in hermeneutics? The answer of Ebeling sounds as perfectly opposite to that of the current opinion; the primary phenomenon of the understanding would not be to understand *the* language, but to understand *through* the language. In which case, a word would not be the "object of understanding," but what allows and mediates the understanding. The word itself is not considered as merely the expression of an individual person, but as a message to be shared (as in the case of love) that needs two human beings; as a communication that with its scope and its point of departure demands experience and brings to experience. The word, in this sense, possesses, according to Ebeling, "a hermeneutical function."[2] Consequently, the object of hermeneutics would be the word-event itself: understanding is possible only where a communication through language is successful, with its arrival and point of departure. If hermeneutics must be the intermediacy of understanding it must reflect on the condition of the possibility of understanding, and thus also on the essence of a word.

---

1 Conference:. Gerhard Ebeling, "Wort Gottes und Hermeneutik" in *ZThK* 56 (1959), pp. 224–251. Translated into English as *Word and Faith* (1963).
2 *Ibid.*, pp. 236–238.

Hermeneutic and demythologizing of the Kerygma 43

As the theory of understanding, the hermeneutics must be a theory of the word, a theory for which the word that discloses the understanding is constitutive in regard to the task of orienting about facts and circumstances. With reference to the Greek language, Ebeling sees in hermeneutics a theory of logos. In fact, the condition of the possibility of understanding is "the immanent logos operating in real things, in the same way than the subject who knows."[3] In conformity with this, he defines the concepts of the theological hermeneutics as "the theory of the Word of God."[4] To this Word, Ebeling recognizes hermeneutical relevance: the specific comprehensive structure of this theology must result from the essential structure of the Word of God. But here the question is: what kind of understanding is realized in this manner? Ebeling asks himself,[5] should the concept "Word of God" be taken in a strict sense as an event of language among humans? (and this is Ebeling's preferred view), or, is "Word of God" a mythic concept, and therefore only of symbolic character with its speech structure being that of mythical speech? Ebeling thinks that the myth as such does not consent a connection with the idea of hermeneutics that has its roots in the Greek concept of logos. In regard to myth, therefore, he concluded that the hermeneutics should become a "demythologizing." However, we ask once again: in case such demythologizing would become indispensable for the understanding, the Kerygma would be, in this way, translated from Divine Word to human word, and thus transformed? At this point, would we not care, as happens in the practice of translations, to try to avoid operating reductions and alterations? In all cases, it would be better to abstain from it, because similar actions imply arbitrariness and presuppositions that are the source of equivocations.[6]

In conclusion, the point we are trying to make is that if hermeneutics must be an intervening mediation to reach the understanding, hermeneutics should not suffer a *reductio ad rationem*, nor an illuminist "rationalization" of the discourse to be interpreted, because otherwise it would not be an interpretation but an evaluative attribution of meaning.[7] Now, two parallel procedures could be mentioned here that are intensified for reasons of practical necessity: on one hand, the biblical text becomes in preaching a helpful hermeneutical means for the understanding of experiences in the present; and in a second instance, the juridical abstract norms become concretized

---

3 *Ibid.*, p. 239
4 *Ibid.*, p. 242.
5 *Ibid.*
6 *Ibid.*, p. 224.
7 On this, cf. *Teoria generale dell'interpretazione*, § 69, pp. 877–885. Cf. Emilio Betti, *General Theory of Interpretation*, Vol. 7, Chapters. 8–9 § 69.

by means of the juridical hermeneutics into a contemporary administration of justice. We will not, however, deal any longer or more deeply with these considerations on hermeneutics, given the practical limitations imposed.

We shall, however, consider the epistemological conditions of the possibility of arriving to an objectivity in the process of interpretation. What has been said on the canon of the actuality of understanding has not exhausted (as Bultmann seems to think) the examination of the hermeneutical directives (the canons) that concern the subject in the interpretation. The spontaneity in the task of interpreting is certainly not to be undervalued; it is not licit in any case to insert it by force and to impose it from the outside of the object to be interpreted, because then the autonomy of the object would be reduced and its knowledge, which, in this instance, is in substance an understanding and a recognizing, could be definitively compromised.[8]

---

8 *Hermeneutisches Manifest*, note 49.

21 Recent turn toward the historicity of understanding

A similar danger is posed not only from the theologians that base themselves on the "demythologizing" of the Christian Kerygma, but also from the few scholars that, under the influence of Heideggerian existentialism, are attributing to the "existential grounding of the hermeneutic circle" the value of a decisive change of direction. For the last ones, the danger is greater, because the new turn toward "*the historicity of understanding*" cannot be reduced or stopped by a delimitation of the functions of competence between historical interpretation and attribution or conferring of an eschatological significance.

A significant book, recently published, offers us the possibility of concentrating on the position of the Heideggerian existentialism in rapport with the historical hermeneutics and of finding a confirmation of the hypothesis just now expressed: Hans-Georg Cadamer, *Grundzüge einer philosophischen Hermeneutik. Wahrheit und Methode*;[1] in which the author's negative point of departure is a sharp criticism of Romanticist hermeneutics and its application to history. We cannot discuss here these criticisms but they seem to be based on a viewpoint that leads to some misunderstandings about Schleiermacher's hermeneutics and to what is, in our view, an unjust assessment. The only positive point that concern us is that Gadamer[2] informs his readers of Heidegger's discovery of the so-called pre-structure of understanding, by means of which he elevates the historicity of the understanding (that is, the historic condition of every process of interpretation) to be the hermeneutical principle, and to arrive to the apparently paradoxical thesis

---

1 For a critical evaluation, see our lecture in Marburg on 22 February 1961 within the frame of *Studium Generale* on the theme "Historische Hermeneutik und Geschichtlichkeit des Verstehens" in this paper. Cf. also our lecture at Bari, 11 April 1961, published in *Annali di Bari*, 16.

2 Gadamer's title "Wahrheit und Methode" from here on will be referred to as *Hermeneutik*, pp. 250–256 (with the successive reference to the English text of "Truth and Method" ed. 1975, pp. 235–241).

that sees in the "prejudices" (*Vorurteile*) "the conditions of understanding." In his view, the primary task of every historical hermeneutics should be the overcoming of the abstract contrast between tradition and events of the past, between history and knowledge of history.[3] The mode of thinking about the living tradition and that of the historical research will together form a unity in which the analysis could discover only the intertwining of their reciprocal influence. Consequently, it would be necessary to recognize in the historian's way of proceeding the actual operative moment of the tradition and to question the hermeneutic productivity. "Understanding is not to be thought of so much as an action of one's subjectivity, but as the placing of oneself within a process of tradition, in which past and present are constantly fused."[4] What follows for understanding from the hermeneutic condition of belonging to a tradition?[5]

---

3 *Ibid.*, pp. 267, 279; ed. 1975 pp. 251, 261–262.
4 *Ibid.*, pp. 274 ff.; ed. 1975 pp. 259 ff.
5 The author asks himself, *Ibid.*, p. 275; ed. 1975 pp. 258–259.

22 The prejudices as the conditions of the understanding

Having underlined the circular kind of relation about the prejudices and the understanding, Gadamer finds the appropriate point of departure in which to insert the consideration of value in the hermeneutical rule, through which one must comprehend the totality in light of the single parts, and the single parts from the whole. The anticipation of a meaning, to which one alludes when speaking of the totality of the tradition, would be thus explicit intelligence that the parts, as they are determined by the whole, determine at their own turn the totality.[1]

Gadamer thinks that "Methodologically conscious understanding would be conceived not merely to form anticipatory ideas, but to make them conscious, so as to check them and thus acquire right understanding from the things themselves." This would be what Heidegger meant when he demanded to "secure" the scientific inquiry by elaborating what previously, by way of anticipation, derived from the objective datum, combining "fore-having, fore-sight, and fore-conception" (and we have here a distorted version of the famous formula of Husserl).

In conformity with this line of thought,[2] Gadamer sees the hermeneutic importance of the temporal distinction in the fact that this distinction forbids the actuality to exercise an excessive influence and will accentuate the authentic meaning, in so far as the distance would be subjected to an infinite process of enlargement. The temporal distinction possesses, in Gadamer's thought, a hermeneutically fecund effect because "it lets prejudices which catch only a part of the work die off, while letting those emerge which

---

1 Gadamer's title "Wahrheit und Methode" from here on will be referred to as *Hermeneutik*, p. 254 (with the successive reference to the English text of "Truth and Method" ed. 1975, p. 239).
2 *Ibid.*, pp. 275 ff.; ed. 1975 pp. 258 ff. Gadamer, in *Heidegger-Festschrift*, pp. 32 ff.; in transl., as *Circle of Understanding*, p. 77.

make possible a true understanding."[3] This means that the interpreter would have to handle constantly the prejudices; the task of hermeneutics would be only that of "distinguishing the true from the false prejudices." A historical conscience hermeneutically educated "will have to make conscious the prejudices guiding understanding so that what is handed down, as a different opinion, stands out and makes itself seen." A prejudice that is present from before but is not conscious, Gadamer adds, "cannot succeed as long as this prejudice is constantly and inconspicuously in play, but rather only when it is, so to speak, stirred up." And "What is capable of this sort of stirring up is the encounter with what is handed down."[4] He, thus, concludes that "whatever entices us to understand has first to have made itself prominent in its otherness." All understanding, indeed, which for Gadamer always means interpretation, begins from the fact that "something speaks to us" (the *Anforderung* in N. Hartmann). When this happens, it involves "a basic suspension of one's own prejudices"; and would raise, from the logical point of view, "a question," the essence of which, for Gadamer, "is to open up possibilities and keep them open." To the historicism that requires the abnegation of the subject, that is of "prescinding from Oneself" and letting Someone Other in our place, Gadamer considers as a "naiveté" the fact of "escaping a dialectical reflection and forgetting its own historicity, while trusting in its method of investigation". Then, he challenges the reader by saying, "Here an appeal must be made from a poorly understood mode of historical thinking to one to be understood more adequately. A truly historical way of thinking has also to keep in mind its own historicity." Finally, he claims that only then the historicity "will it give up pursuing the phantom of a historical objectivity – which is subject of a continually advancing research – learning instead to recognize in the object the Other of its Own, therewith bringing to recognition the One and the Other."[5]

We could try to confute the dialectical proceeding proposed by Gadamer with the arms of the Hegelian dialectics, but our interest stands only in showing that a loss of objectivity at which the doctrine of Gadamer would arrive, cannot in any possible way be compensated by the acquisition of conscience of one's own historicity acquired by the subject. The criterion by him proposed for the discernment of true prejudices from the false ones – a criterion of exactitude called "fore-conception of completeness of the object" – is based on an auto-deception, that is, it is a criterion that cannot be trusted for the validity of the results in the interpretative process.

---

3 Gadamer, in *Heidegger-Festschrift*, p. 33; in transl., as *Circle of Understanding*, p. 78.
4 *Ibid.*
5 *Ibid.*, p. 34; in transl., as *Circle of Understanding*, p. 79.

23 Existential foundation of the hermeneutic circle

We want now to take a close look at Gadamer's development of thought.[1] The provisory "expectation of meaning" on the part of the interpreter of a text should be accordingly well formulated as the text requires. "The anticipation of meaning in which the whole is envisaged becomes explicit understanding in that the parts, that are determined by the whole, themselves also determine this whole." In this way, "the movement of understanding is constantly from the whole to the part and back to the whole" in a circular process of reciprocal illumination. The task should be "to extend in concentric circles, the unity of the understood meaning. The harmony of all the details with the whole" would be "the criterion of correct understanding."[2] At this point, Gadamer states that "the task of hermeneutics is to clarify this miracle of understanding, which is not a mysterious communion of souls, but a sharing of a common meaning," adding that "the goal of all communication and understanding is agreement concerning the object"[3] that is a content-related agreement. Here he affirms a fundamental and inherent contrast between the ideal of the objectivity dreamed by Schleiermacher, who would neglect to assign value in his theory on hermeneutics to the concrete historical conscience of the interpreter and to *the existential foundation of the hermeneutic circle* of Heidegger, who talks of it as of "a decisive turning point."[4] In the theory of Schleiermacher, an interpreter's acts are the means by which one places oneself entirely within the writer's mind and from there resolves all that is strange and unusual about the text. "As against this approach, Heidegger describes the circle in such a way that the understanding of the text remains permanently determined by the anticipatory movement of fore-understanding." The anticipation of meaning

---

1 Gadamer, *Hermeneutik*, pp. 275–279; ed. 1975, pp. 258–263.
2 Thus thinks Gadamer, *ibid* p. 275; ed. 1975, pp. 258–259.
3 *Ibid.*, p. 276; ed. 1975, pp. 259–260.
4 *Ibid.*, p. 277; ed. 1975, pp. 261–262.

that governs our understanding of a text "proceeds," in Gadamer,[5] "from the communality that binds us to the tradition" and "is contained in our relation to tradition, in the constant process of education." From this point of view, the hermeneutic circle would describe "an ontological structural element in understanding." And the consequence is that every effort to understand would be conditioned by the presupposition that "only what really constitutes a unity of meaning is intelligible."[6]

Gadamer preferred to call this presupposition, which guides and conditions all understanding, "pre-conception of completion" (or, better, perfection of the text).

---

5 *Ibid.*
6 *Ibid.*, p. 278; ed. 1975, p. 262; Gadamer, *Heidegger-Festschrift*, p. 30.

24 The problem of the correctness of the understanding

Now, it seems to us that the evidently feeble point of the hermeneutical method proposed by Gadamer would consist in the fact of truly allowing an agreement between the text and the reader – that means a correspondence between the meaning of the text that presents itself in appearance as obvious and the subjective personal conviction of the reader – but in no way warrants the *correctness* of the understanding. For this, it would be necessary that the reached understanding would conform in a fully adequate way to the objective meaning of the text as an objectivation of the spirit. Only in this way could it be said that the objectivity of the result is assured on the basis of a reliable process of interpretation. It is not difficult to demonstrate, on the contrary, that the instance of objectivity escaped the method proposed, and that in substance the method is uniquely intended to achieve the interior coherence and completion of the meaning that was supposedly to be accepted, and, for this purpose, it would be sufficient to consider carefully the suggestions formulated by the Author itself. When we read the texts – Gadamer says – we begin from the presupposition that they are finished, that is, complete; but when this presupposition is not respondent or is insufficient, then it reveals that the text is not intelligible and, thus, we should question the incomprehensible text, and "we start to doubt the transmitted text and seek to discover in what way it can be remedied"[1] in order to arrive at the understanding of the textual content.[2] Thus, the presupposition of the "fore-conception of completion," that is programmed by the author, could demonstrate itself always determinable in function of the

---

1 Gadamer, *Hermeneutik*, p. 278; ed.1975, pp. 262–263; Gadamer, *Heidegger-Festschrift*, pp. 30 ff.
2 It seems that it is a manner of proceedings that is at risk; it tends to compromise the philological objectivity of the text, and could be taken as legitimate only as a critique of what has been said (*Kritik des Richtigen*) in the sense of Droysen (*Historik*, 1937, § 32, pp. 122–131).

content. In this way, "an immanent unity of meaning guiding the reader assumed, but his understanding is likewise guided by the constant transcendent expectation of meaning which proceed from the relation to the truth of what is being said."[3] On the contrary, according to the author, "It is only when the attempt to accept what is said as true fails" that is needed to "try to 'understand' the text, psychologically or historically, as another's meaning." Therefore, "the fore-conception of completeness" would then include not only "this formal element that a text should fully express its meaning" (that is, with clarity and precision), "but also that what it says should be the whole truth."[4] Thus spoke Gadamer.

His manner of presenting the hermeneutic question presupposes, then, that the interpreter charged with the task of understanding is pretending to have the monopoly of the verity, if not as an acquired possession, at least as a power of a checking device. To the contrary, our mode of seeing is that the interpreter should limit itself to the reception of the thought of someone else as it is expressed in a text as an alien opinion, and letting it speaks, even when erroneous views are manifested in it. Gadamer himself[5] must after all admit undoubtful exceptions to the hypothesized fore-conception. For example, in the case of a disarranged or codified piece of writing (*Verstellung*), in which the dissimulation of the text is not otherwise more noticeable than with the previous intelligence of the text in light of the key that explains its intelligence and comprehension. However, if we reflect that the language used by humans contains habitually an overflow of meaning, because of its constant elliptic character, then the actual fact is that we do not say all that we presume to be known, as a logical or axiological premise of the discourse: we are therefore obliged to renounce to the hypothetical presupposition of completeness, and to generalize the exception.

Concerning the place to be assigned to the historical interpretation, Gadamer[6] makes no differentiation between the position of the legal historian and that of the jurist, which must study its application, because he misreads the fundamental diversity of the orientation of the historian from that of the jurist, and in reference to the present, he pointed to the juridical hermeneutics as "the model for the relationship between past and present that we are seeking,"[7] and that on this model the historical sciences should keep their eyes. Gadamer truly conceded that the historian who wants to

---

3 This too would be an interference of the critique of exactitude that should come up questionably in the conclusion of the interpretive process.
4 This would be like having the prejudice of the "*Kyriolexia*" confuted by Schleiermacher (*Hermeneutik* in *Werke* I/VII, p. 133).
5 Gadamer, *Hermeneutik*, p. 278, note 2; ed. 1975, p. 263.
6 *Ibid.*, pp. 308–310; ed. 1975, pp. 289–293.
7 *Ibid.* p. 311; ed. 1975, pp. 292–293.

ascertain the historical importance of a law[8] cannot disregard the fact that he is concerned with a legal creation that needs to be understood in a legal way.[9] But he would also want to see in the particular case of the historian, which occupies itself with a legislative text with a vigor still valid in contemporary time,[10] the model that "shows us what determines our relationship to any historical tradition." He says, "The historian, trying to understand the law in terms of the situation of its historical origin, cannot disregard the continuance of its legal validity: it presents him with the questions that he has to ask of historical tradition." Very well, but these queries are only the consequential and far-removed effects that have necessarily no influence on the present and that, in any case, must not determine the practical attitude of the historian concerning the present, nor to influence directly on its taken stance. Thus, to the queries that Gadamer[11] reconnects afterward to these assertions, we must complexly respond in a negative manner. He asked himself, "Is this not true of every text, that is, that it must be understood in terms of what it says?" And, "Does this not mean that it always needs to be restated?" And, again, "does not this restatement always take place through its being related to the present?" Our responses are a resolute "No!" It is nonetheless true that when the creative process reverses itself into the interpretive process, then a relocation of meaning from the original perspective of the author[12] to the subjectivity of the interpreter is certainly necessary. The relocation is not a "transplantation" that, reaching us, speaks into the present and must be understood in this mediation, indeed, "as this mediation with the present." The time we call "the present" increases and stimulates the noetic interest for the understanding, but in the "transplantation" the *subjective stance* of the *speaking subject* remains excluded from it. The conceptual equivocation that insinuates itself in the argumentations that we saw is expressed, in my opinion, in the

---

8 This is valid for any content of the historical tradition; cf. on the topic: Rothacker, "Dogmatische Denkform in den Geisteswissenschaften und das Problem des Historismus" in *Abhandlungen der Akademie d. Wiss. und Literatur*, 1954, pp. 249–258, 261-263; cf. ours *Teoria generale della Interpretazione* (1955), § 37c, p. 599. Cf. Emilio Betti, *General Theory of Interpretation*, Vol. 4, Chapter 5, § 37c.

9 That is, in the sense of the juridical dogmatics. Against S: Gadamer, *Hermeneutik*, p. 309; ed. 1795, p. 291.

10 It is a case that Gadamer, in *Hermeneutik*, p. 308, ed. 1975, pp. 290-291, had presented previously as the only possible one.

11 *Ibid.*, p. 311; ed. 1975, p. 293.

12 From "the subjective stance" of the "speaking subject," according to the English expression of E. D. Hirsch Jr., "Objective Interpretation", in *Publication of the modern language - Association of America*, year 75, n. 4 (part I: September) pp. 463–479, especially p. 476.

reasoning that follows.[13] The object of the historical understanding would not be the events, but their meaning (in reference to the present), that is, their significance for the present time.[14] Consequently, this understanding would not be conceived in an exact way by those who, postulating the objectification as a datum existing in itself, affirm that the interpreter has the duty of going on approaching it.[15] In truth, it would be in the essence of the historical understanding (so conceived) to presuppose a tradition still operative within the living actuality, so that the understanding necessarily would have to base itself on the mediation of the past and the present; even better, as the same *mediation of past and present*.

---

13 Gadamer, *Hermeneutik*, p. 311; Ed. 1975, pp. 292–293.
14 Symptomatic here appears the agreement of Gadamer with the argumentation of Bultmann.
15 "Hermeneutisches Manifest," p. 123; here note 63.

25 Historical understanding as mediation of past and present

If things are the way we have seen, then the case of juridical hermeneutics should not be a particular case; it would be rather capable of render to historical hermeneutics all its wide field of problems and to restore the ancient unity of the hermeneutic problem, in which the jurist and the theologian associate with the philologist. But things are not so. It has been told to the jurists by the radically different attitude that is required from them when from the juridical applications we move to consider in a merely theoretical way the history of law and rights. The hermeneutic necessity of understanding the propositions of a text by going back to its original concrete situation[1] implies, for the legal historian, nothing more than a teleological evaluation on the obligation of expressing such propositions into a precept, carefully ascertaining that the evaluation would have no immediate, in reference to the present, normative influence on the contemporary kind of comportment.[2] In reality, the reference to the present has for the historian a total different meaning.

Even the conclusion of Gadamer[3] which derives the exigency, valid for him, in a way for the historian differently than for the philologist, of interpreting the tradition in a diverse sense from what the texts *per se* would say, of searching behind the texts, and beyond the intention expressed in texts, the reality that they involuntarily and unconsciously reveal – seems debatable. All of this, even though today the philologist is requested to frame the texts in a wider context, and though its rapport with the texts depends also on the oscillations resulting from a model that implies a continuation and a certain application.[4] Gadamer sees the historian to be approaching the texts (as historical sources) like an inquiring judge listening to witnesses; this judge would regulate itself with the shown historical testimonies in the

---

1 Gadamer, *Hermeneutik*, p. 317; ed. 1975, pp. 298–299.
2 To such topic, *see* our "Hermeneutisches Manifest," here note 123.
3 Gadamer, *Hermeneutik*, pp. 319-321; ed.1975, pp. 301–303.
4 *Ibid.*, p. 321; ed. 1975, p. 303.

same way than any other judge would deal with the depositions of the testimonies of a trial. "In both cases a testimony" would be "an aid in establishing the facts," but in the second case the facts would not be "the real objects of enquiry; they are simply material for the real tasks of the judge, to reach a just decision, and of the historian, to establish the historical significance of an event within the totality of historical self-consciousness."[5]

Thus, all of the difference could be reduced to a simple question of size! The properly decisive elements, meanwhile, would pre-exist in each employment of the historical methods. The author sees the problem of the "*application*" – thanks to a singular equivocation of the intentions of what the text intends to say[6] – appearing determinant also for the most complicated case of the understanding of the history, which would be against any appearance.

All reading[7] "involves application so that the person reading a text" would be "himself part of the meaning he apprehends. He belongs to the text that he is reading." In this way, the author grasps the interior unity of history and philology, not for what concerns the historical critique of the tradition as such, but basically for the fact that both operate an application that is different for each because of its measure. All that is needed for this, Gadamer says, is to recognize that "the unity of the hermeneutical disciplines comes into its own again if we recognize that effective historical consciousness is at work in all the hermeneutical activity of both critic and historian"!

---

5 *Ibid.*
6 *Ibid.*, p. 322; ed. 1975, p. 304.
7 So Gadamer thinks, *Ibid.*, p. 323; ed. 1975, p. 304.

26 Claim of a practical application of interpretation

The historians with all the guardians and practitioners of historical hermeneutics, who are concerned about the objectivity of their task of interpretation, are called upon to oppose such a presumptuous self-assertion of subjectivity that would demote the process of the historical interpretation to a mere mediation-of and to a confront between past and present. The analogy here presumed of the historical hermeneutics with the juridical-normative hermeneutics is in reality based on a self-deception. The application of the law requiring an interpretation oriented in function of the needs of the life of relationship of the present time is a necessary result from the scope proper of the law considered as the ordering of the co-existence in a human community. It is part of its essence, then, that it should achieve a concretion of the law,[1] that is an *application*, in so far as it provides to the life and the conduct of the community a practical guide and directives conforming with justice. The same reasons are valid also for the exegetical interpretation of the sacred texts of the theologian, because of its orienting and normative tasks; the faithful ones are expecting, from this exegetical interpretation, an *application* in morality that would influence their practical comportment.[2]

---

1 K. Engisch, *Die Idee der Konkretisierung in Recht und Rechtswissenschaft unserer Zeit*, Heidelberger, Akademie, 1953, pp. 96ff.
2 This is the place for the concept of "application": Wach, *Verstehen*, II, pp. 19ff. On this, also Ebeling, in *ZThK*, 1956, p. 249; cf. the above Chapter 20 titled "Theological Hermeneutics and Demythologizing of the Kerygma."

27 The mentioned claim is justified only if the interpretation is normatively oriented

All this is, however, quite different in the case of historical interpretation, which cannot enjoy the same treatment as that of the normative interpretation of jurisprudence and theology. Its task is purely theoretical. Its interest is the verification of the meaning, in itself already concluded, of a fragment of the past. In its case, the remote and the proximate effects of the historical events to be questioned must be evaluated in conformity with the canon of the totality with the due detachment of the historian. Here, there is not at all a question of transposition into the present time. On the other side, the proceedings themselves with which the research was made of the mediation between past and present – such as the transposition into the present, the appropriation, the assimilative adaptation, the interpretative conversion of meaning, and the transformation of an unintelligible tradition – have characterized an anti-historical attitude toward the past. In addition, no matter how fecund could have been the misunderstandings when animated by the effort to valorize the structures of the past as "practical implements of life,"[1] they, too, failed. The productive integration, surely, the transposition, and the evolutional renewal are all applications of the past to the present; they are certainly useful and stimulant for the life of the society. They are justifiable within the domain alone of our living and practicing together.

We must, however, with decision and strength deny their legitimacy and justification from the point of view of the dimension here in question, that is, the question of the historical hermeneutics. The mentioned proceedings are manifestly unsuitable to reveal the historical reality and they are rather opening the doors to the subjective *arbitrium*, tending to hide the truth of history, and sometimes also distorting, and unconsciously deviating it. The historian who has become conscientious of the

---

1 "Problem der Kontinuität im Lichte der rechtshistorischen Auslegung" (*Inst. Mainz*, 18, 1957), pp. 30 and 40.

historicity of its own understanding would abstain from these proceedings, and would take its distance from "the practice of the applications."

Everyone who has exercised in concrete any historical research would very well know that the critique in relation to the sincerity and the reliability of the historical testimonies fully appertain to a completely other dimension.

It is the honorable duty of an interlocutor to avoid concluding its own critical observations without expressing to its partner in the dialogue its own honest thankful acknowledgments for the suggestions and the stimulations received. Every scientific critique conscientiously done brings the two partners in the dialogue to enrich themselves with self-criticism and knowledge of oneself. Even when we could succeed to illumining the adversary and to bring it to its self-reflection, we also obtain involuntarily the advantage of having being changed and induced to better know ourselves, as well. In a frontal meeting we should not conduct ourselves as being in a hard battle, but rather balance our influence with the one that is proposed in what we are told.[2]

With a free disposition of spirit, we must wait for the ulterior developments announced by Professor Gadamer and that will appear in "*Philosophische Rundschau*."[3] We are grateful to him and to our common friend, Walter

---

2 F. Nietzsche, *Die fröhliche Wissenschaft,* § 321.s

We wish therefore to conclude our modest critique with a personal confession. When, 34 years ago, in Milan, we were giving a prolusion on the role of the modern juridical dogmatics in the juridical-historical interpretation, our principal preoccupation was that of demonstrating such function as legitimate and necessary, and that the demonstration from this methodic point of view was based on the historicity of understanding. What was important to us especially was, in opposition to the traditional views, to accomplish in this field a Copernican turn, in a Kantian sense. That meant to maintain the awareness of the part that the subject has in the cognitive process of the sciences of the spirit and to place in the right light how in its meeting with history it is historically determined. We must still today coherently affirm the historicity of understanding and recognize that the understanding itself is an inexhaustible task, and that it changes with the position of the historian in its own time. In this fundamental point we are in agreement with both colleagues Bultmann and Gadamer, and they must consider us as like-minded with them and grateful for their strong accentuation of the role of the interpreter in the interpretive process. In one only thing, we do not agree with them. We do not agree with their doctrines of the pre-understanding and of the justification of the prejudices because they make problematic the objectivity of the understanding, and with it the scientific nature of the results of the interpretation. Nonetheless, we are far from the ridicule presumption to decree from our restricted angle that it is possible to have perspectives on hermeneutics only from this angle (cf. Nietzsche, *Die fröhliche Wissenschaft,* §. 374). On the contrary, our divergent approaches to hermeneutics could be valued as single paths equally concentric included in the immense universe of knowledge of the sciences of the human spirit.

3 While the article "Hermeneutik und Historismus" was being published in *Philosophische Rundschau,* 9 (April 1962), pp. 241–276.

60 *Interpretation is normatively oriented*

Hellebrand, for the clarifications received from their correspondence. Their friendly explanations are precious because they illustrate the germ and the dominant motive of the new philosophical hermeneutics.[4] Anyway, for a

---

4 In his friendly letter of 18 February 1961, Prof. Gadamer wrote,
'Fundamentally, I am *not proposing a method*, I am describing *what is the case*. That it is as I describe it cannot, I think, be seriously questioned. ... You, for example, know immediately when you read a classic essay of Mommsen the only time when it could have been written. Even a master of the historical method is not able to keep himself entirely free from the prejudices of his time, his social environment, and his national situation, etc. Is this a failing? And even if it were, I regard it as a necessary philosophical task to consider why this failure always occurs wherever anything is achieved. In other words, I consider the only scientific thing is *to recognize what is*, instead of starting from what ought to be or could be. Hence, I am trying *to go beyond* the concept of method held by the modern science (which retains its limited justification), and to envisage in a fundamentally universal way what *always* happens. ...' You are perfectly right when you say that the principle of 'completeness' is not a criterion of truth. It is precisely also what I think. Even more, I think that this is much part of the 'prejudices' of the understanding, often misleading, even though unavoidable. Then, when there is a positive need of knowledge, we must overcome this prejudice. In this only way, a critique is still possible when facing what seems guaranteed. Criticism, however, is not normally present in our act of understanding. Criticism is subjected to definite conditions that, at their turn, presuppose an auto-affirmation of understanding. In that same measure, the presupposition of completeness is what *begins to function as the guide*. This is as much as I had been thinking about the topic.'

The result from this sincere and precious confession, it is here, using the Kantian formulation, a *quaestio iuris* concerning "what must be done" that is transformed in a *quaestio facti*, in which the problem is not that of legitimation of certain interpretive proceedings, but of their factuality.

From his own side, Prof. Walter Hellebrand notices in his letter of 6 April 1961, that the principal preoccupation of Gadamer is, as it seems, that of bringing the interpreters to become aware of the historicity of their work, of the actuality of their understanding, and thus of their being immersed in the tradition, and of inexhaustive nature of the hermeneutical task. The more interpreters become conscious of the historicity of their understanding, the more – he thinks – they will avoid to follow the phantasma of an unreachable historical objectivity, and much better they will be aware of the interdependence of the knower and what is known. The position of Gadamer is against "isolationism" and it is clarified by his conception of the play (pp. 97ff.) and especially by his conception of the totality (inseparability) of the play and of the partner in a play (cf, on the topic, Eugen Fink, *Spiel als Weltsymbol*, Kolhammer 1960). The cognitive process for Gadamer is a game, with subject and object together mediated by some means, that is, for instance, instruments or measures of any kind, or symbols of thought, or systems of mathematical equations, or method of research, and "antennas" of any type. Knowledge (through its cognitive means) aims at overcoming the subject-object transcendence, and especially the temporal distance; everything is a means for knowledge, that is, it is everything that, according to the preparation of the subject itself, its profession, etc. (and in particular, the language), ties the subject to the text and involves the interdependence of subject and object.

correct formula of presentation of the question it is necessary to notice from the beginning that the epistemological problem – using the exemplary formula of Immanuel Kant in the *Critique of Pure Reason* – is not a *quaestio facti*, but a *quaestio iuris*. It is concerned with a problem of justification which does not aim at ascertaining what actually happens in the activity of thought apparent in interpretation, but which aims at finding out what one should do, that is, what one should aim for in the task of interpretation, what methods to use, and what guidelines to follow in the correct execution of this task. Therefore, after our critical excursions, let us return to our examination of the hermeneutic canons.

This explains how, in order to overcome the temporal distance, students' study carefully all the hermeneutical attempts used previously on a text, attempts that are also utilized in their heuristic values by the interpreter in the present. No less than a Savigny, with his studies on the Justinianic and actual Roman law, have repeatedly – following the incitements of Hugo! – underlined the necessity of a historical-dogmatics research of a problem, from Tribonianus through the Glossa until the post-glossators, and then up to the humanists and the following practitioners of the *usus modernus pandectorum*. Model of it is his book on "possession." Instructive is also his Preface to *System of the Modern Roman Law,* of which there exists also an English translation. It is unfortunate that the most recent pandectists and the critics of interpolation have disregarded almost completely to care for the history of the influence of the classical ideas in the Middle Ages and in the Modern Epoch.

How difficult it is today to penetrate in the ideal world that is at the base of the law of the ancient Greece, or also of the Acadian and Sumerian juridical institutions! On the contrary, the Old Testament law of the Talmud, the ancient Germanic and medieval rights, and their rich "history of effects" are for us heuristic subsidies.

Critical of the point of view of Gadamer is E. Kuhn, "Wahrheit und geschichtliches Verstehen" in *Historische Zeitschrift*, 193, 1961, pp. 376ff. A conciliatory position of the problem is proposed by O. Kohler, "Historiker und Kulturmorphologen" in *Saeculum* 12, p. 311, which is set up on a presumed inseparability of past and present, and it is a presumption that, in my view, could guide into several misunderstandings.

28 The canon of the hermeneutical correspondence of meaning (Adequation of meaning in understanding)

If it is true that only the human spirit speaks to another spirit, then it is also the case that only a spirit at the same level and congenially disposed can communicate with the human spirit that speaks to it and is able to understand in an adequate manner what is said. An actual interest for understanding, no matter how much alive it is, for establishing the required communication, is not enough. A spiritual open-mindedness is needed that would allow the interpreter to collocate itself in the just and most favorable perspective for its investigation and understanding.[1] We are speaking here of the disposition of an ethical and theoretical reflective human spirit, that could be negatively defined as unselfishness and humble self-effacement, as they are manifested in the sincere and decisive overcoming of personal prejudices, and some real attitudes that are eventually contrasting with an understanding that has not been previously informed.[2] The same human spirit can be also defined positively as with a broad viewpoint and wide horizon and wealth of interests: the ability of assuming toward the object of the interpretation a congenial attitude animated by a sentiment of strict affinity.[3]

This needed ability has been what evidently has inspired the *fourth* canon of hermeneutics, which connected as it is with the third, of which we have already spoken, focuses also on the subject of the interpretation. We prefer to call it the canon of *adequation of meaning in understanding*, or canon of *hermeneutical correspondence of meaning* (that is, of the hermeneutic consonance). According to this canon, the interpreter should strive to bring its own lively actuality into the closest adhesion and harmony with the message that it receives from the object in such consonant way that the one and the other resonate in harmony and perfect unison.

---

1 *Hermeneutisches Manifest: Zur Grundlegung einer allgemeinen Auslegungslehre*, note 50.
2 *Ibid.* note 51.
3 *Ibid.* note 51a. See our *Teoria generale dell'interpretazione*, § 13, pp. 269–282 (or Emilio Betti, *General Theory of Interpretation*, Vol. 2, Chapters 2 and 3, § 13).

This aspect of the canon of correspondence of meaning is especially apparent in the field of the historical interpretation where it was for the first few times noticed by common observation.[4] It is here that the datum of individuality, as is verifiable in a historical personality, should vibrate with the personality of the interpreter, if it is to be *recognized* by the latter.[5] If it is true that the historical personality manifests itself as an unity in the mode and grade in which some representative contents unify in a conscience,[6] then the proper congenial empathy with such mode and grade of synthesis is one of the condition that permits the interpreting historian to recreate from within that specific personality.

The *canon of consonance of understanding,* in the way that we think of it, is in itself of an universal importance and embraces all kinds of interpretation.[7] If, however, we prefer to consider the historical interpretation, we will find two possible aspects: first, the interpretation of the sources and of the relics of a historical tradition; second, the interpretation of the comportments on which, in conformity with the formulation of the historiographic problem by the researcher,[8] an effort has to be made to focus on the historical interest, with the interpellation on the life of single individuals or of social communities. A distinction is at this point needed whether the inquiry on the historical material and the evaluation of the problematic aspects of the social life in the past are conducted by means of categories that can be psychological, practical, ethical, or political – as in the case of biography, political history, or history of customs and morality (Ethos) – or, perhaps, the inquiry and the historical evaluation may demand that we would consider the character as a *work* of the forms of life in question, which should then represent a higher problematics.

---

4 *Hermeneutisches Manifest: Zur Grundlegung einer allgemeinen Auslegungslehre,* note 52.
5 *Ibid.,* note 58.
6 *Ibid.,* note 58a.
7 *Ibid.,* note 59.
8 *Ibid.,* note 105.

29 The character as a work of historical forms of life

Proposes a problematics of the higher grade

The second case is present when the historical analysis of the structures focuses on such objects as the artistic creations in their various forms: the works of literature in their different types and genres; the science in its various branches; the formations of law; the economic systems; and the social and religious organizing forms of societies and communities. Every time that these kinds of cultural levels, which are realized by human beings in the life of their communities, become the object of the structural analysis in history, then, this is the time for the process of interpretation of a piece of history, which is part in the history of civilization, and requires a more precise hermeneutical problematics of a higher order. The hermeneutical problematics configures itself, at various times, in many different ways in the history of art, language, literature, science, jurisprudence, social structures, economic and religious structures, but for reason of the character as a *work* proper to these forms of life, the relative problematics in their diverse fields confers to the interpretation a type of communal dynamics that is clearly distinguished from the generically historical interpretation.

The objects of this type of interpretation are representative forms that, as it has been said, have a firm character as a *work*, that must be approached, in its multiple structures, as appertaining to the history of the civilization and of the human spirit. In order to succeed in characterizing the type of interpretation of which we speak we must return to a distinction in the theory of hermeneutics, a distinction noticed, and for the first time accurately examined, by the great Schleiermacher,[1] but that successively fell into oblivion. In the field of the psychological interpretation, widely studied, Schleiermacher indicated a difference between the psychological inquiry strictly considered and the technical inquiry. Schleiermacher intended to apply the adjective "technical" to hermeneutical inquiry in the strict sense of an expressive technique, the technique of expression in a literary work – that is, the

---

1 *Hermeneutisches Manifest: Zur Grundlegung einer allgemeinen Auslegungslehre*, note 108.

technique that oversees the reflection (meditation) and the construction (composition) of these works – and that he does not intend them in the wider sense of semantic technique or technique of representation, which can refer to any kind of significative production outside the field of the written language. In addition, it is clear that in the field of interpretation the technical, that is the *morphological*, moment, in rapport with the limited acceptation (of meaning), involves a more important role and would need a much wider application. If, in fact, we admit every act of understanding to proceed from the inversion of an act of speaking and thinking, in which the question is of running over again retrospectively the course of the thoughts that are at the base of the discourse and of arriving at their comprehension, it would be clear that from the process of inversion we can extract a general principle of correspondence of meaning between the creative process of a product of the human spirit and the effort of its interpretation. One then recognizes the deep truth of Giambattista Vico's[2] statement that, "The civil world is certainly the creation of human kind. And, consequently, the principles of the civil world can and must be discovered within the modifications of the human mind."[3] Verily, the multiple and typical configurations that the human civilization assumes in the course of its historical development within the variety of the cultural systems and in the various spheres of the spiritual human life – art, language, literature, science, law, economic and social structures – each one possesses a *logos* of their own that is both law of formation and development, at the same time, a law of a structure with a "nexus of meaning." In the light of this law, then, an interpretation is possible for understanding the sense of these cultural products, keeping in mind the single problems of their formation, according to typical factors that recur in them and also the individual factors, both historically conditioned.[4]

2 *Ibid.*, note 109. On this topic, see our lecture "I princípi di *Scienza Nuova* di G. B. Vico e la teoria dell'interpretazione storica" in *Nuova Rivista di Diritto Commerciale*, 10, 1957, pp. 48–59 (or Emilio Betti, *The Principles of New Science of G. B. Vico and the Theory of Historical Interpretation*, E. Betti's Lecture at the University for Foreigners in 1957).
3 *Hermeneutisches Manifest,* note 110. G. B. Vico, *The New Science*, Translated by David Marsh. Penguin Books, pp. 119–120, §§ 330–334.
4 *Hermeneutisches Manifest,* note 110a.

30 The technical-morphologic interpretation in rapport to the prospected problems of formation

One could call such an interpretation that regards the various cultural works as solutions to *morphological* problems of formation – even though the artist itself may not have been aware that there was such a problem – a *technical* interpretation with a historical task, if one wanted to use Schleiermacher's criterion and expression. It would be more appropriate, from the point of view of the contemporary use of language, to call this kind of interpretation "morphological" (Fritz Wagner has recently suggested the term).[1]

When one person speaks of "technique" in rapport to the history of civilization, this person certainly and usually thinks uniquely of the progress of the material civilization, without including in the concept, at the same time, the higher forms of the objective spirit.[2] We find ourselves then to face, here, an arbitrary limitation. A technique that intends to discover the single laws that oversee the formation of the various works of the life of the spirit and of the social cultural systems of which the human civilization nourishes itself:

> this technique could be used in the kind of interpretation that would want to recognize and reconstruct from the inside such products in their generation and formation, in their style, in the inner coherence of their structure and in their conclusiveness, and which attempted to give an over view of the historical development of styles.[3]

If the evaluations dominant in consecutive stylistic epochs constitute a spiritual horizon regulated by a perspective historically conditioned and circumscribed, then it is sufficiently clear to admit that the modes of feeling, conceiving, and visualizing, not only in the language, but also in all other

---

1 Wagner, *Archiv für Kulturgeschichte*, 38, 1956, p. 261.
2 *Hermeneutisches Manifest*, note 110b.
3 *Ibid.*, note 110c.

spheres in the life of the human spirit – as long as they are not subordinated to over temporal and immutable categories – are governed by hermeneutical categories, which, radically mutable from time to time in function of historically determined conditions, pertained to the rapports between human beings and the external world.[4] At this point, the problem that confront the historian consist in finding out if the manifold changes in conceptions, representative modes, feeling and thinking, theories and dogmas, institutions and structures are following a developmental law and would submit to tendencies of treatment that would consent to a phenomenological manifestation (a clue),[5] especially when it is about tendencies in which a sequence of different styles is recognizable.[6]

At the level of an objective spirit, in reality, some laws of development are operating that cannot be reconstructed with an interpretation that is merely psychological. In the history of arts, literature, sciences, legislations, and economic and social systems, the historical datum is not limited to an experience purely individual of given personalities; it consists rather in an essence that *contains some values*, that is, it is charged by a content of meaning, of a value and of a character of *creative work,* of which is required an understanding, beginning from ourselves, the intimate unity of style and the strict correlation of their meaning with other values and other equal works, independently from the circumstances conditioning their historic emergency and from the nexus merely chronological between "before" and "after." In view of ascertaining the historical derivation and of underlining the essential line of the development that characterizes a sequence of operative models, a preliminary exigency is activated that understands the character as a *work*, the conception, the structure within the peculiar logic by which the product is objectively shaped, and to reconstruct the concatenation of the participant ideas and of the representative contents into which the product seems articulated.[7]

To orient correctly the historical knowledge after the examination of the sources on the cultural values they represent, what is needed exactly is the proposed technical-morphological interpretation, for the reason that it inclines to see in the various works of imagination, thought, and action the solution of problems that could, in a wide sense, define morphologic problems, or of conformation. In this way, it succors a technical-artistic interpretation of the works in the visual arts, in order to elaborate a history of the various arts under the profile of the respective problems of

4 *Ibid.,* note 113.
5 *Ibid.,* note 114.
6 *Ibid.,* note 114a.
7 *Ibid.,* note 119.

expression.[8] In an analogous case, it helps a linguistic-scientific or technical-literary interpretation of written works for the construction of a history of language and of literature, according to the various linguistic fields and the diverse literary genera, to which, in spite of the accusations made toward them, they must nonetheless be well recognized as a function of orientation, in so far as they correspond to different types of a linguistic communication determined by the direction and the goal by which the activity of communication itself is formulated, that is, to make others to share in one's own personal thoughts.[9] Again, some analogous considerations are valid for the technical-scientific interpretation of the history of law, economy, and sociology. Equally useful for a history of the scientific problems in the different fields of knowledge is an interpretation of doctrines and systems; analogically, even a technical-juridical interpretation that operates with the conceptual instruments of dogmatics, with a historical-juridical orientation, according to the criteria of the internal logics of the juridical formations and fundamental principles of the law itself. Finally, it serves a technical-sociological interpretation, or even a technical-economic one, of social and economic systems for the history of the social and economic structures.[10] The task to be accomplished in this is that of acknowledging the traditionally constant rapports between historical data, even if chronologically remote among them, trying to group them around specific morphological problems of the social life, emergent in the correlative environments of inquiry, according to points of view that respond to a precise interest of the historian and of the comparative research.[11]

In this way, therefore, the experts of the various sciences of the spirit will elaborate, through the technical-morphological interpretation, hermeneutical guiding concepts and ideal models that they could use for the comprehension of the history of the multiple expressions of the human civilization considered as the history of problems of formation and history of solutions of problems that preside over the genesis and the development of works and structures.[12] Now, we limit ourselves to mentioning two precursors and their works for your enjoyment and profit: Heinrich Wölfflin, *Kunstgeschichtlike Grundbegriffe* and Emil Staiger, *Grundbegriffe der Poetik*.[13]

---

8 *Ibid.*, note 119a.
9 *Ibid.*, note 120.
10 *Ibid.*, note 120a.
11 *Ibid.*, note 121. Concerning this, see O. Kohler, "Die Historiker und die Kulturmorphologen" in *Saeculum* 12, 1961, pp. 306-318; A. Hilckmann, "Geschichtsphilosophie, Kulturwissenschaft, Sociologie" in *Saeculum, ibid.*, pp. 405-420.
12 *Hermeneutisches Manifest,* note 122.
13 On this, *see* also K. Goldammer, *Die Formenwelt des Religiösen* (1960).

31 Context of meanings and styles as products of the autonomy of the spiritual human faculties

Only a fine and educated artistic sensibility and an adequate preparation can help the interpreter, to whom the expressive problems of art are familiar because of a personal experience, to unfold those problems that the work of art has resolved, perhaps even in a partially unconscious mode, and to understand the meaning-content. Equally, only a jurisprudent's intelligence, to whom, thanks to its experience and preparation, the intellectual instruments of the legal dogmatics are familiar, can position the historian of law in the condition of facing the problems of the genesis of all the instituted principles of law and of the juridical conceptions, in which the problem is consisting in separating from the structure of theoretical institutes the function they assumed within the course of time.[1] Only the mind of the sociologist that has reflected on the morphological problems of the organization of the social life places the historian of civilization at the level of fully and completely clarifying those typical factors constantly recurrent and the evolutive tendencies that sustain the changes of the social structures in the running of history; and makes a community able to live in a given environment and to react normally in an identical manner to equal situations of power and living.[2] The experts of ancient literatures and the historians of classic antiquity proposed a similar need, when they wished in our time to elaborate an archaeological hermeneutics that would take as its object the products of the figurative representations (sculpture and painting), with the finality of recognizing and reconstructing, by overcoming their immediate semantic value, these representative forms in the overflow of meaning of their images, with the help of an interpretive integration derived from literary texts.[3]

1 *Hermeneutisches Manifest,* note 123. *See* our lecture, "Jurisprudenz und Rechtsgeschichte vor dem Problem der Auslegung" in *Archiv für Rechts und Sozialphilosophie* 40, 1952, pp. 364ff.
2 *Hermeneutisches Manifest,* note 124.
3 *Ibid.,* note 125.

Only the theologian, who is able to do more than just perceive external or internal changes, would, in a similar way, understand the internal evolution of religions and with the characteristic ability of historians follow the becoming of the representative forms and of their vectors and intuit the laws that regulate the dialectics of the becoming, submitting to a general normativity, though stepping in the direction of an individual law.[4]

It is always a question of issues that present a historical interest, but of a nature that cannot be explored and understood exhaustively by the usual ethical and psychological categories. In these similar matters or representative contents, the technical-morphological interpretation can satisfy the need of the adequation of meaning of the understanding or of the hermeneutic correspondence that explores in proximity the overflow of meanings of the cultural creations and constitutes, as we have seen, one of the fundamental canons of hermeneutics. It is the duty of the historian of art, language, and literature, as well as of the historian of law, economy, and religion, but also of the sociologist, the task of comprehending the work of art, the institutions, the typical compartments, in their own internal coherence and validity, in their nexus with the representative forms and the similar types, and of underlining their "*style*," which is the product of autonomous spiritual powers. In that way, the technical interpretation becomes an analysis of the structures of representative content, but also an analysis that reveals to us its character as a *product,* and explains how ever something that is appears so neatly distinct as valid and not-valid by an evaluating critique, in light of a technical-morphological examination, appears instead united and more or less equally justified in force of a substantial communion of aspects. It is also possible to consider here individual works or products of the collective human spirit, and the interpreters could look at what their own formation and competence on the argument permit them to discover, that is, what they have assimilated in the authentic meeting with the literary, the artistic, the juridical, and the religious works. Divergent interpretations always teach us that any authentic and organically elaborated work of art is fully alive within its own stable boundaries. Let us then remember the imperishable truth enunciated by Johann Wolfgang Goethe: solely in its togetherness can humanity properly have the full knowledge of the work of one human being.

It is a fact that the subjective spirit of a single human being could be raised up to the heights and led down into the depths by the forms of the spiritual objectifications that remain unapproachable to its own experience, because these forms are located beyond the horizon of its limited autonomous

---

4 So, approximately, J. Wach in *Archiv für Rechts und Sozialphilosophie* 40, 1952, pp. 372 ff.

capacity to experiment. Profundity, elevation, amplification, and enrichment are experienced by the interpreter on its way to the understanding, and they clearly differ from what a conscience reaches in the course of its own immanent development. The essential moment is the fact that what grasps us in its purity and depth is an objectified significant content, a matter of overflowing spirituality. The advantage that we can derive from artworks of great value for our own formation and self-education is one thing; another is the experience that these masterpieces provoke in us in the cosmos of the objectifications of the spirit, objectifications having significative contents of which we recognize the superiority in rapport to our subjectivity, and that we arrive at understanding, not so much with our forces, but because they raise us up to higher levels. In the same way as primitive human beings carried with themselves the fetish's magical virtues which could overcome their forces, so the civilized humans find themselves surrounded by works infinitely greater than they could be.[5]

If we could conceive the totality of the significative forms on the whole constituting the unity of the total human civilization, we would then have an idea of the tension of familiarity and unfamiliarity, tension that acts in the entire dialectical rapport between the subjective spirit and the objectivized spirit. A given human being can very well try from time to time to take possession of the entire production of the past, but then it must recognize that the patrimony of thought accumulated by the immense labor of so many generations carries in itself significant contents that, though being works of the human beings, have a significance that transcend them. It can be said that the knowledge of history and the knowledge of oneself correspond in a peculiar mode.[6] In the essence of this process of knowledge of oneself there must be the fact that the human spirit can run through this path or course to its end only because it establishes with the significative contents *a confront* that springs from life as something other than itself, something objective, something higher. Only by pulling with strength our crossbow toward the significative contents we make possible the countereffort of our spirit for the knowledge of oneself so that the historical knowledge is not only the path of the human being toward itself, but is at the same time the road toward that higher something that, according to the great maxim of Goethe, greatly transcends the single individual human being.[7]

---

5 Freyer, *Theorie des objecktiven Geistes*, p. 87.
6 This for a recent Bultmann, *Geschichte und Eschatologie*, p. 137; *History and Eschatology*, p. 122. But previously this idea of auto-conscience and auto-education was anechoically expressed by Nietzsche, *Menschliches, Allzumenschliches,* II, p. 223 (cf. 208, 292; *Der Wanderer und sein Schatten* 188–189. Also, Droysen, *Historik*, p. 168).
7 Freyer, *Theorie des objektiven Geistes*, p. 88.

Autonomy of the spiritual human faculties

With this, in the field of the entire science of the spirit, the common general hermeneutical problematics emerges that configures itself in a differentiated manner in its application to diverse branches. To those thinkers dedicated to these sciences, we limit ourselves to the fact of having offered a simple notice about their possibility.[8]

---

8 At last, allow me, to refer to our *Teoria generale della interpretazione,* especially Chapter 5: "Interpretazione Tecnica in Funzione Storica," §§ 30–38-a. (or. Emilio Betti, *General Theory of Interpretation*, Vol. 4, Chapter 5, §§ 30–38-a.).

Index

Note: Page numbers followed by 'n' refer to notes

abolition of objectivity 40–41
Acadian and Sumerian juridical institutions 61n4
actuality of understanding xiv, xv, 21
analogy and integrative development 19–20
anticipation of perfection xvii, xx
antinomy 12–13
archaeological hermeneutics 69
Aron, Raymond Claude Ferdinand 1

Bedeutsamkeit 33
Bedeutung 33
Betti, Emilio xi–xxv, xxvii, 16n1
Betti–Gadamer debate xi–xxv
Boeckh, August 1, 2n1
Bultmann, Rudolf 21, 22n5, 23, 23n8, 25, 26, 26n2, 27, 32n1, 33n4, 33n6, 34n1, 37, 38, 42

canon of adequacy xiv–xv
canon of consonance of understanding 63
canon of totality xiii–xiv, 16–18
Celsus, Publius Juventius 16
cognitive power of spirit 36
coherence 16–18
Coing, Helmut 1, 2n1
Collingwood, Robin George 1, 38
compartments 7
concept of "application," 57, 57n1
concept of conferring 36
conceptual equivocation 54

contemporary consciousness 1–2
content-related agreement 49
creative process 12–13
Crifò, Giuliano xxvi
"the criterion of correct understanding," 49
criticism 60n4
Critique of Pure Reason 61
cultural actual evolution 31

Davidson, Donald xxii
demythologizing of Christian Kerygma 42–45
dialectical proceeding 48
dialog and monolog 34–35
Dilthey, Wilhelm xi, xxii, xxvii, 1, 2n1, 18
direction of inquiry 22–24
divergent interpretations 70
Droysen, Johann Gustav 1, 30, 33n5
Dworkin, Ronald xvi
Dworkin's interpretivism xv–xvi

Ebeling, Gerhard 37n3, 42, 43
Engisch, K. 57n1
epistemological conditions 44
epistemological problem 61
eschatology 36, 37
existential encounter with history 30
expectation of meaning 49
expressive value 7–8

Festschrift für E. Rabel 2n1
figurative expression 4
fore-conception of completeness 48, 52
fore-conception of completion 51
fourth canon of hermeneutics 62
Frank, Erick 23n6
Freyer 33n3, 71n5, 71n7

Gadamer, Hans-Georg xi–xxv, xxvi, 30n1, 45, 48, 50, 51, 52, 52n5, 53, 53n10, 54n13, 55, 55n1, 55n3, 60n4
Geschichte und Eschatologie 22n4, 23n8
Giambattista Vico's² statement 65
Goethe, Johann Wolfgang 70, 71

Hartmann 36n1
Hartmann, N. 2n1, 48
Hegelian dialectics 48
Heidegger 49
Heideggerian existentialism 45
Heidegger's discovery 45
Hellebrand, Walter 59–60, 60n4
hermeneutical disciplines 56
hermeneutical function 42
hermeneutical problematics 1–2, 64
hermeneutical procedure 40
hermeneutic autonomy xiii, 14–15
hermeneutic task 32
Hermeneutisches Manifest 32n2
historical-dogmatics research 61n4
historical hermeneutics 55, 57
historical interpretation 63
historical personality 63
historical phenomenon 25–26, 32–33
historical question 30
History and Eschatology 22n4, 23n8
Hobbes, Thomas xv, xvi, xix
Humboldt, Wilhelm von 1, 2n1, 9, 10

illation 7
intellectual instruments 69
intelligence and comprehension 4, 5, 9, 52
interlocutor 59
interpreter 22, 26
interpretive process 9–11
inversion 12–13
isolationism 60n4

Joh, Körner 37n4
juridical hermeneutics 53, 55, 57
jurisprudence 17–18

Kantian formulation 60n4
Kant, Immanuel 61
Kaufmann, Fritz 26
Kerygma 42–44
Kuhn, E. 61n4

Lazarus, M. 2n1
legal norms 19
linguistic communication 68
Löwith, K. 40n1

Marrou, Henri-Irénée 1
mediation of past and present 54
Mohr, J.C.B. xxvi–xxvii
movement of understanding 49
musical expression 4

Niebuhr, Reinhold 1
Nietzsche, F. 37, 59n2
normative interpretation of jurisprudence and theology 58

objectification of spirit 4, 10–11
objective knowledge 25–26
object of understanding 42
ontological structural element in understanding 50

paradoxical thesis 45–46
phenomenological manifestation 67
philosophical hermeneutics 60
Pinton, Giorgio A. xxvi–xxvii
positive law xviii–xix
practical implements of life 58
pre-conception of completion 50
prejudices 46, 47–48
presupposition 51
problem of irrationality 27n1
productive integration 58

radical interpretation xxii
Ranke, Leopold von xii, 1
reciprocal illumination 16–17
representative function 5–8, 14

Romanticism 1
Romanticist hermeneutics 45

Savigny, Friedrich Karl von 1
Schlegel, August Wilhelm 1
Schleiermacher, Friedrich xi, xxii, xxvii, 1, 2n1, 16, 17, 52n4, 64
Schleiermacher's hermeneutics 45
scientific hermeneutics xvi
settlement-function xxiv
Simmel, Georg 1, 2n1
spiritual commonality 5–6
spiritual human faculties 69–72
spiritual open-mindedness 62
Steinthal, H. 2n1
subjectivist orientation 40
System of the Modern Roman Law 61n4

technical-artistic interpretation 67
technical-morphological interpretation 66–68, 70

teleological evaluation 55
Teoria generale della interpretazione 2n1
theological hermeneutics 43
theory of Schleiermacher 49
triadic process 10–11
Truth and Method xix

value judgment 28
value-relating interpretation 27–29
Verbum Dei ut viva vox 37
Vinx, Lars xi–xxv

Wach, Joachim 2n1
Wagner 66n1
Weber, Max xx, 28, 29, 29n2
Wölfflin, Heinrich 68
Word of God 43

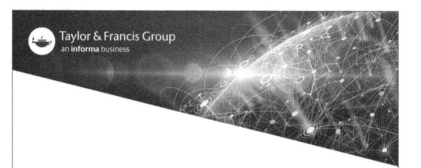